COLLOQUIAL
SPANISH

By

WILLIAM ROBERT PATTERSON
F.R.G.S., F.R.A.S., M.R.A.S., F.R.A.I., M.C.P., Etc.
Author of 'Colloquial French'

Revised and brought up to date by

G. H. CALVERT
M.A.

ROUTLEDGE & KEGAN PAUL
LONDON, BOSTON, MELBOURNE AND HENLEY

First published 1919
Second Edition (with a few corrections) 1922
Third Edition (revised and reset) 1931
Reprinted nine times
Fourth Edition (revised and reset) 1963
Reprinted 1969, 1970, 1974, 1979, 1981 and 1983

Published by Routledge & Kegan Paul plc
39 Store Street, London WC1E 7DD
9 Park Street, Boston, Mass, 02108, USA
296 Beaconsfield Parade, Middle Park,
Melbourne, 3206, Australia and
Broadway House, Newtown Road, Henley-on-Thames, Oxon RG9 1EN

© Routledge & Kegan Paul Ltd 1963

ISBN 0 7100 4325 2 (c)
ISBN 0 7100 6385 7 (p)

Printed in Great Britain by Redwood Burn Limited,
Trowbridge, Wiltshire

PREFACE TO THE REVISED EDITION

THE basic pattern of the previous edition has been largely re-tained, and the purpose of the book remains the same, to enable the student to acquire fairly rapidly a knowledge of the elementary structure of spoken Spanish. The use of the word 'colloquial' in the title is not intended to indicate that this is a handbook of 'colloquialisms' or popular phrases, but that the emphasis is on everyday spoken Spanish rather than on the literary language.

The grammatical sections have been considerably augmented, in the belief that real progress demands a thorough knowledge of grammatical principles, and a table of irregular verb conjugations has been added as a second appendix. Spelling and accentuation have been amended to satisfy the latest requirements of the Royal Spanish Academy. The book makes no pretensions to complete-ness, but it contains enough basic material to form an adequate groundwork for more advanced study of the language.

1963   G. H. C.

CONTENTS

SCOPE OF LESSONS

I

INTRODUCTORY REMARKS

COMPARATIVELY, the Spanish tongue is not a difficult one to acquire. The pronunciation is simple, following fixed rules, and the accidence and syntax, in a broad sense, will present very few stumbling-blocks. In questions of advanced style all languages, of course, become complicated in their construction. This point, however, may be dismissed for the time being, since we are to learn the idiom from the beginning and in its simplest form at first in order to prepare a solid foundation for the more difficult work later.

The student of Spanish is fortunate in having ready at his command a fairly extensive vocabulary, due to the resemblance of many Spanish words, in both orthography and meaning, with English ones.

I select any Spanish work at random from my book-case and encounter, in the opening pages, the following words, which the reader will recognize and understand at once, even though the spelling may not be, in every case, exactly that of English—

volumen	literatura
moderno	valor
principal	extenso
público	personal
autor	existir
clásico	oficial
idea	horror
compatriota	actual
vital	silencioso
indirecto	filósofo
último	atmósfera
amoroso	literario

1

Most English words ending in '-ion' have '-ión' in Spanish—

consideración	publicación
investigación	explicación
definición	generación
cuestión	porción
acción	repulsión
habitación	concepción
creación	indicación
observación	emoción
manifestación	impresión
sensación	importación

The English substantive ending '-ty' is usually found in Spanish as '-dad'—

sinceridad	austeridad
idealidad	realidad
generosidad	temeridad
ciudad (*city*)	tranquilidad
universidad	

The suffix '-ly' of English adverbs becomes in Spanish '-mente'—

profundamente	momentáneamente
frecuentemente	generalmente

The foregoing are but a few instances of the close relationship between the English and Spanish tongues; there are hosts of others. If the student will scan the columns of any Spanish periodical he will discover dozens of words strongly resembling English ones; it remains for him to master the intervening words, the purport of which he, as a beginner, will, of course, not understand.

This quick recognition of likeness will give him very little assistance in speaking the tongue, though the knowledge that his work is, to a great extent, simplified will, without doubt, tend to encourage him. Few of the Spanish words I have chosen as examples would be understood by a native of Spain if they were pronounced by a Briton who knew no Spanish. The explanation is that both our vowels and consonants have sometimes other values than are found in Spanish, and vice versa, as I will show in the chapter dealing with pronunciation. The student who learns a foreign language merely for the purpose of reading is depriving himself of manifold pleasures, and will never attain originality; there is as much fascination in speaking and writing as in reading.

Now, it is quite a simple matter to grasp the signification of some words by studying the context, but it is by no means easy to recall a word at any given moment. It requires, therefore, very little effort to read and comprehend what one reads. The question of speaking and writing is entirely another matter, and demands a certain degree of fluency on the student's part, which can be obtained only by constant repetition. By constantly repeating a word or phrase it becomes absorbed by the brain without any effort of will and can generally be recalled instantly. Hundreds of expressions that are stored away somewhere in our brain-cells have been retained there by constant repetition. One of the secrets of modern advertising lies in bringing certain words, phrases or illustrations continually before the eye of the public. It is, indeed, a very successful method.

Consider, for a moment, the number of advertisements which you can remember having seen at various periods of your life. We have no reason to memorize these things, yet it is inevitable that we should do so, for they are thrust upon us at every turn— in our periodicals, at the railway station, on moving vehicles, and on walls. The result of this constant repetition is clear; we memorize what we see by what may be termed a process of gradual absorption. By such a means we are less likely to forget than if we taxed the brain heavily over a short period. This is the best of all systems to adopt in the study of modern foreign languages, and even those words which resemble English words in their orthography must be treated in the same way. A large vocabulary is of little value unless it can be used for purposes of reading, writing, and speaking. I do not intend this work to be a complete guide to the Spanish tongue, for there exist so many already, and, moreover, my purpose would not be served by so doing. I propose only to teach the colloquial idiom with such idiomatic expressions as may be encountered in daily speech.

An augmented vocabulary will only be necessary after the reader has mastered the contents of this book.

Many beginners, in their efforts to speak like a native but overcome by their own enthusiasm, imagine that rapidity of utterance tends to render their meaning clearer; but this is quite a misguided idea and does not constitute fluency. A man may be a fluent speaker, though a slow and deliberate one; on the other hand, another may declaim with great speed and yet make no pretence to fluency on account of the poorness of his grammar. It is rarely necessary to speak hurriedly. The following advice is quoted from Chapter I of *The Bible in Spain*, by George Borrow, first published in 1843:

'Those who wish to make themselves understood by a foreigner in his own language, should speak with much noise and vociferation, opening the mouth wide. Is it surprising that the English are, in general, the worst linguists in the world, seeing that they pursue a system diametrically opposite? For example, when they attempt to speak Spanish, the most sonorous tongue in existence, they scarcely open their lips, and putting their hands in their pockets, fumble lazily, instead of applying them to the indispensable office of gesticulation.'

Language-study ought never to be forced, yet one should concentrate all one's thoughts upon the lesson while it is in progress, and this can usually be done without tiresome effort.

The amount of labour entailed in learning a foreign language is as nothing compared to the benefit an intelligent individual may reap from such knowledge, for it not only brings its own reward as an asset to one's education, and, incidentally, to one's profession, but it also provides an admirable training for the brain in any other work it may be called upon to do.

Now, take this book with you on your walks into the country and read aloud as you go. This is the healthiest form of study.

Take it with you into the garden, on your daily journeys to and from your place of business, and on your holidays, and read either aloud or silently, even for a brief period. Remember that every odd minute is of value. Strive to cultivate persistency, and if you cannot go forward with your work, do not, on any account, fall behind. When you do not feel sufficiently energetic to undertake the study of a new chapter it would be a wise plan to read over the back work. There should be a frequent revision of all that has been done, for this forms the foundation of one's knowledge, and it is quite evident that one's progress depends upon the soundness of the elementary work. Do not imagine, because a Spanish word resembles its English equivalent, that less notice should be taken of it, but learn it as carefully as you do the rest, giving special attention to its pronunciation.

II

PRONUNCIATION

THE following indications are only approximate. To pronounce Spanish properly, and particularly to acquire the correct intonation, the student should whenever possible listen to Spaniards, to broadcasts in Spanish, or to recordings in the language.

The Vowels

A midway between *a* in *hat* and *a* in *father*.

E like *e* in *empty* before two consonants, otherwise resembling *a* in *hate*. It is never mute.

I like *i* in *routine*.

O like *o* in *sole*; but before two consonants and in some mono-syllables it has a shorter sound, resembling *o* in *off*.

U like *u* in *rule*, but it is mute after *q*, and after *g* unless marked with the diaeresis (*e.g.* lingüista).

Y equivalent to Spanish *i*.

It should be noted that the sound of Spanish vowels is unaffected by their being preceded or followed by another vowel. Thus, **aire** should be pronounced as **a–i–re**, **sois** as **so–is**, **reuma** as **re–u–ma**, etc.

The Consonants

B like English *b* but less explosive.

C before *e* and *i* is pronounced like *th* in *think*, otherwise like *c* in *cast*.

As English *th*	As *c* in *cast*
cebra (*zebra*)	caballo (*horse*)
cera (*wax*)	codo (*elbow*)
cerveza (*beer*)	cuatro (*four*)
cigarro (*cigarette*)	cuchara (*spoon*)

6

CH like *ch* in *church*.

D like English *d*, but at the end of words or between two vowels it has a softer sound resembling *th* in *then*.

F as English *f*.

G before *e* and *i* is pronounced gutturally, like the Scottish *ch* in *loch*; otherwise like *g* in *good*.

H is always mute.

J is pronounced gutturally like Scottish *ch* in *loch*.

K as English *k*.

L as English *l*.

LL as *li* in *valiant*; thus 'millón' is pronounced rather like the English 'million' with the stress on the 'o'.

M as English *m*.

N as English *n*, but *nv* is pronounced as *mb*.

Ñ as *ni* in *onion*; thus, 'niño' is pronounced 'neenyo'.

P as English *p*, but less explosive.

QU as English *k*.

R is rolled, similarly to a Scottish *r*; at the beginning of a word it is equivalent to *rr*.

RR is strongly rolled.

S like *s* in *same*.

T as English *t*.

V as Spanish *b*.

X as English *x* before vowels, as *s* in *same* or as *egs* before consonants.

Y as English *y*.

Z as *th* in *think*.

The student should note particularly that *CH*, *LL*, and *Ñ* are separate letters of the Spanish alphabet. When using a dictionary he will find words beginning with *LL*, for instance, in a separate section between *L* and *M*; to take another example, 'falla' appears after 'falúa'.

Stress and Accentuation

Spanish words ending in a vowel, *n*, or *s* are stressed on the penultimate syllable. Words ending in a consonant other than *n* or *s* are stressed on the final syllable.

Penultimate	*Final*
muchacho (*boy*)	verdad (*truth*)
martes (*Tuesday*)	mujer (*woman*)
inmediatamente (*immediately*)	veloz (*swift*)
ventana (*window*)	corral (*corral*)
protestan (*they protest*)	carey (*tortoiseshell*)

When the stressing of a word does not follow these rules a written accent is used to indicate the stressed syllable:

fácil (*easy*)	habitación (*room*)
lápiz (*pencil*)	carácter (*character*)

A, E, and O are termed strong vowels, and two of them together constitute two syllables. I and U are termed weak vowels; when one of these precedes or follows a strong vowel a diphthong is formed, and the strong vowel is the stressed one, unless the weak vowel has a written accent. When two weak vowels are together the second is stressed, unless the first has a written accent.

Two strong vowels together	*Strong vowel with weak vowel*	*Two weak vowels together*
maestro (*master*)	pausa (*pause*)	ruido (*noise*)
leamos (*let us read*)	luego (*then*)	viuda (*widow*)
caoba (*mahogany*)	tierra (*land*)	flúido (*fluid*)
	oímos (*we hear*)	
	reíamos (*we were laughing*)	

As well as indicating an irregularly stressed vowel, the written accent is placed over the stressed syllable of interrogatives and exclamatory words, and serves to distinguish between words spelled alike but with different meanings. The most common of these are the following:

mi = *my*	mí = *me*
tu = *your*	tú = *you*
el = *the*	él = *he*
si = *if*	sí = *yes; himself, etc.*

se = *himself, etc.*   sé = *I know*
te = *yourself, you*   té = *tea*
de = *of; from*   dé = *give* (present subjunctive of *dar*)
mas = *but*   más = *more*
solo = *alone*   sólo = *only*

Punctuation

A peculiarity of Spanish is to precede questions and exclamations with an inverted question mark or exclamation mark:

¿Dónde está usted?   = Where are you?
¡Qué día tan hermoso! = What a beautiful day!

Capital letters are slightly less common in Spanish than in English. For example, they are not used for days of the week, months, seasons, or in nouns and adjectives denoting nationality:

enero   = January
lunes   = Monday
un español = a Spaniard

It is usual to introduce conversations with a dash, and the equivalent of inverted commas (*comillas* « ») is generally reserved for quotations.

III

THE FIRST LESSON

SPANISH nouns are either masculine or feminine, and their respective definite articles are 'el' (masc.) and 'la' (fem.). The article 'lo' is used with adjectives and possessive pronouns having an abstract sense.

el libro	= the book
la casa	= the house
lo bueno	= the good
lo mío	= mine (what belongs to me)

The indefinite articles are **un** (masc.) and **una** (fem.).

un libro	= a book
una casa	= a house
una manzana	= an apple

With very few exceptions, nouns ending in **o** are masculine and those in **a** feminine.

Masculine		*Feminine*	
el tío	= uncle	**la tía**	= aunt
el hermano	= brother	**la hermana**	= sister
el cuchillo	= knife	**la pluma**	= pen
el cuadro	= picture	**la mesa**	= table

The commonest masculine words ending in **a** are—

el poeta	= poet
el guardia	= policeman
el monarca	= monarch
el día	= day
el tema	= theme, subject
el clima	= climate
el programa	= programme

10

The commonest feminine words ending in **o** are—

> **la mano** = hand
> **la radio** = radio
> **la moto** = motor bike
> **la foto** = photo

There are a few words ending in **a** which are of common gender, such as:

> **el** (*or* **la**) **periodista** = journalist
> **el** (*or* **la**) **artista**   = artist
> **el** (*or* **la**) **comunista** = communist

A few feminine nouns, beginning with a stressed **a** or **ha**, take the masculine article in the singular only.

> **el agua**   = water
> **el hacha** = axe
> **el águila** = eagle
> **el alma**   = soul
> **el hambre** = hunger

The best plan to adopt in learning the Spanish nouns is to repeat the article with each one, associating the one with the other. It should be noted, however, that nouns ending in **-ción** and **d** are feminine.

> **la ciudad**   = town, city
> **la salud**   = health
> **la lección** = lesson
> **la sociedad** = society
> **la pasión**   = passion
> **la nación**   = nation

Nouns ending in an unaccented vowel form their plural by adding **s**. Nouns ending in a consonant add **es**.

Singular		*Plural*	
el amigo	= friend	**los amigos**	= friends
la amiga	= friend	**las amigas**	= friends
el hombre	= man	**los hombres**	= men
la mujer	= woman	**las mujeres**	= women
un libro	= book	**unos libros**	= books
la ciudad	= town	**las ciudades**	= towns
el árbol	= tree	**los árboles**	= trees
el color	= colour	**los colores**	= colours
una rosa	= rose	**unas rosas**	= roses
la lección	= lesson	**las lecciones**	= lessons

Note that whenever a substantive ends in **z** this letter changes to **c** before **es** is added, as—

la luz = light **las luces**

Also, most nouns which end in a vowel carrying a graphic accent add **es** to form the plural, as—

el rubí = ruby **los rubíes**

The position of the graphic accent does not change.

Exceptions are a few words taken from French:

el papá	= father	**los papás**
la mamá	= mother	**las mamás**
el sofá	= sofa	**los sofás**

The verbs 'to be' and 'to have' present some difficulty, as there are in Spanish two words for each.

to be = (1) **ser**; (2) **estar**

In general, **ser** is used before noun complements, with adjectives denoting permanent characteristics, and with past participles to form the passive.

Yo soy soldado	= I am a soldier
mi tío es rico	= my uncle is rich
la puerta es abierta	= the door is opened

Estar indicates position and temporary states, and is used with past participles when the latter serve as adjectives.

> **Madrid está en España** = Madrid is in Spain
> **yo estoy enfermo** = I am ill
> **la puerta está abierta** = the door is open

> To have = (1) **tener;** (2) **haber**

Of these verbs, it will suffice to say that **haber** is used as an auxiliary verb to form compound tenses—

> **yo he estado** = I have been
> **yo había visto** = I had seen

whereas **tener** is used in all other cases implying possession—

> **yo tengo un libro** = I have a book

Present Indicative

	haber	tener	ser	estar
I	yo he	tengo	soy	estoy
you	tú has	tienes	eres	estás
you	usted ha	tiene	es	está
he	él ha	tiene	es	está
she	ella ha	tiene	es	está
we	nosotros hemos	tenemos	somos	estamos
you	vosotros habéis	tenéis	sois	estáis
you	ustedes han	tienen	son	están
they	ellos han	tienen	son	están
they, *f.*	ellas han	tienen	son	están

It will be noted that there are four pronouns for 'you'. **Tú** and its plural **vosotros** are familiar forms. The polite or formal mode of address is **usted** (singular) and **ustedes** (plural). These pronouns are frequently abbreviated in writing to **Vd.** and **Vds.,** and are used with the third person of the verb.

Note also that **nosotros** and **vosotros** have feminine forms **nosotras** and **vosotras.**

A short vocabulary follows which will help the student to a better understanding of the phrases which succeed it, and which are to be considered as a foundation for the more comprehensive sentences in later chapters. Do not turn over any page until you have mastered all that is contained therein. All the work in this book is so graduated that no page should prove truly difficult if the past vocabularies and rules and exercises have been honestly treated.

VOCABULARY

bueno	= good (*masc.*)	ni —— ni	= neither —— nor
buenos [1]	= good (*masc. plur.*)	no	= no; not
el caballero	= gentleman, sir	la señorita	= young lady, miss
la tarde	= afternoon, evening	el periódico	= newspaper
la casa	= house	el libro	= book
esta	= this (*fem.*)	el padre	= father
de	= of	el perro	= dog
de la	= of the (*fem.*)	sí	= yes
de las	= of the (*fem. plur.*)	no —— sino	= only
muy	= very	contento	= pleased
gracias	= thanks	mucha (*fem.*)	= much
el edificio	= building	muchas (*fem. plur.*)	= many
el teatro	= theatre	porque	= because
un señor	= a gentleman, sir	nada (no —— nada)	= nothing
buena	= good (*fem.*)	la madre	= mother
buenas	= good (*fem. plur.*)	rico (rica)	= rich
el día	= day	el sombrero	= hat
la noche	= night	llamar	= to call
este	= this (*masc.*)	llamarse	= to call oneself
esto	= this (*neut.*)	¿cuánta (*fem.*)	= how much?
del	= of the (*masc.*)	¿cuántas (*fem. plur.*)	= how many?
de los	= of the (*masc. plur.*)	la hija	= daughter
¿cómo?	= how?	yo sé	= I know
bien	= well	pero	= but
¿qué?	= what?	creo	= I believe
el palacio	= palace	la verdad	= truth
		sino	= but
		mucho (*masc.*)	= much; a lot of

---

[1] Adjectives agree, in gender and number, with the nouns they qualify.

muchos (*masc. plur.*)	= many	me	= myself, me
¿por qué?	= why?	¿cuánto (*masc.*)	= how much?
mi	= my	¿cuántos (*masc. plur.*)	= how many?
el hermano	= brother	el hijo	= son
la hermana	= sister	la mujer	= woman; wife
pobre	= poor	Vd. sabe	= you know
el amigo	= friend	la edad	= age
se	= him, her, it, your, one (self), your, them(selves)	el año	= year

The numbers from one to twenty are:

1	uno (una, *f.*)	11	once
2	dos	12	doce
3	tres	13	trece
4	cuatro	14	catorce
5	cinco	15	quince
6	seis	16	dieciséis *or* diez y seis
7	siete	17	diecisiete *or* diez y siete
8	ocho	18	dieciocho *or* diez y ocho
9	nueve	19	diecinueve *or* diez y nueve
10	diez	20	veinte

From twenty-one onwards thus—

21	veinte y uno (veintiuno)	200	doscientos (doscientas, *f.*)
30	treinta	300	trescientos (trescientas, *f.*)
40	cuarenta	400	cuatrocientos (cuatrocientas, *f.*)
50	cincuenta	500	quinientos (quinientas, *f.*)
60	sesenta	600	seiscientos (seiscientas, *f.*)
70	setenta	700	setecientos (setecientas, *f.*)
80	ochenta	800	ochocientos (ochocientas, *f.*)
90	noventa	900	novecientos (novecientas, *f.*)
100	ciento	1,000	mil
101	ciento uno	1,000,000	un millón

Uno shortens to **un** before a masculine noun—

un hombre = one man

Ciento shortens to **cien** before a noun—

	cien hombres	= a hundred men
	cien casas	= a hundred houses
but	**ciento una casas**	= a hundred and one houses

The ordinal numbers are:

1st	**primero**	11th	**undécimo**
2nd	**segundo**	12th	**duodécimo**
3rd	**tercero**	13th	**décimotercero**
4th	**cuarto**	14th	**décimocuarto**
5th	**quinto**	15th	**décimoquinto**
6th	**sexto**	16th	**décimosexto**
7th	**séptimo**	17th	**décimoséptimo**
8th	**octavo**	18th	**décimoctavo**
9th	**noveno (nono)**	19th	**décimonono**
10th	**décimo**	20th	**vigésimo**

From the twentieth onwards thus—

21st	**vigésimo primero**	70th	**septuagésimo**
30th	**trigésimo**	80th	**octogésimo**
40th	**cuadragésimo**	90th	**nonagésimo**
50th	**quincuagésimo**	100th	**centésimo**
60th	**sexagésimo**	1,000th	**milésimo**

When expressing the date, cardinal numbers are used for all but the first of the month—

el primero de enero	= the 1st of January
el dos de mayo	= the 2nd of May
el veinticuatro de junio	= the 24th of June

el lápiz	= pencil	**yo hablo**	= I speak
medio	= half	**Vd. habla**	= you speak
viejo	= old	**¿dónde?**	= where?
aquella (*fem.*)	= that	**mal, malo** (*masc.*)	= bad
también	= also	**la naranja**	= orange
en	= in	**el primo** (*masc.*)	= cousin
inglés	= English	**el soldado**	= soldier
francés	= French	**joven**	= young
me gusta	= I like	**aquel** (*masc.*)	= that

aquellos, aquellas (pl.)	= those	hablar	= to speak
		él habla	= he speaks
se dice	= it is said, one says	lo	= it
		mala (fem.)	= bad
español	= Spanish	solamente	= only
alemán	= German	la prima (fem.)	= cousin
gustar	= to please		

CONVERSATIONAL MATTER

Buenos días, señor	= Good morning, sir.
Buenos días, señor Castelar	= Good morning, Mr. Castelar.
Buenas tardes, señorita	= Good evening, miss.
Buenas noches, señora	= Good night, madam.
¿Qué casa es ésta?	= What house is this?
Es la casa del señor González	= It is Mr. Gonzalez' house.
¿Cómo está Vd.?	= How are you? (How do you do?)
Muy bien, gracias	= Very well, thank you.
¿Qué edificio es éste?	= What building is this?
Es un teatro	= It is a theatre.
¿No es un palacio?	= Isn't it a palace?
No, señor, no es un palacio	= No, sir, it is not a palace.
¿Tiene Vd. un libro?	= Have you a book?
No, señorita, no tengo ni libro ni periódico	= No, miss, I have neither book nor newspaper.
Mi padre tiene dos perros	= My father has two dogs.
¿Es verdad?	= Is that so? (Is it true?)
Sí, es verdad	= Yes, it is true.
Mi madre tiene tres gatos	= My mother has three cats.
Yo no tengo sino uno	= I have only one.
Estoy muy contento	= I am very pleased.
¿Por qué está Vd. contento?	= Why are you pleased?
Porque tengo mucho dinero	= Because I have a lot of money.
Mi hermano no tiene nada	= My brother has nothing.
¿No tiene nada?	= He has nothing?
No, pero mi hermana tiene mucho dinero	= No, but my sister has a lot of money.

¿Es rica, la hermana de Vd.?	= Is she rich, your sister?
Sí, pero mi hermano es pobre	= Yes, but my brother is poor.
¿Qué es eso?	= What is that?
Es un sombrero	= It is a hat.
¿Quién es este caballero?	= Who is this gentleman?
Es mi amigo	= He is my friend.
¿Qué tiene él?	= What has he?
No tiene nada	= He has nothing.
¿Tiene Vd. algo?	= Have you anything?
Sí, tengo este periódico	= Yes, I have this newspaper.
¿Quién es este hombre?	= Who is this man?
Es mi vecino	= He is my neighbour.
¿Es rico?	= Is he rich?
No, es muy pobre	= No, he is very poor.
¿Cómo se llama Vd.?	= What is your name?
Me llamo Juan	= I am called John.
¿Cómo se llama este hombre?	= What is this man's name?
Se llama Pedro	= His name is Peter.
¿Tiene él una hermana?	= Has he a sister?
Tiene cinco	= He has five.
¡Qué hombre!	= What a man!
¿Por qué?	= Why?
Porque habla cinco lenguas	= Because he speaks five languages.
¿Cuántas hermanas tiene Vd.?	= How many sisters have you?
No tengo sino una	= I have only one.
¿Cuántos hijos tiene esta mujer?	= How many sons has this woman?
No sé	= I don't know.
¿Cómo, Vd. no sabe?	= What, you don't know?
No, pero sé que tiene una hija	= No, but I know that she has a daughter.
¿Es guapa la hija?	= Is she pretty, the daughter?
Sí, señor, es muy guapa	= Yes, sir, she is very pretty.
¿Qué edad tiene ella?	= How old is she?
Creo que tiene dieciséis años	= I believe that she is sixteen years old.

¿Cuántos años tiene esa señorita?	= How old is that young lady?
No tiene sino catorce años y medio	= She is only fourteen and a half.
Es muy joven	= She is very young.
Mi padre es muy viejo	= My father is very old.
Y mi madre también	= And my mother also.
¿Cómo se dice 'nine' en español?	= How does one say 'nine' in Spanish?
Se dice 'nueve', señor	= One says 'nueve', sir.
¿Y cómo se dice 'nueve' en alemán?	= And how does one say 'nueve' in German?
No sé, señor	= I don't know, sir.
¿No sabe Vd. el alemán?	= Don't you know German?
No, señor, porque no me gusta	= No, sir, because I don't like it.
¿Habla Vd. francés?	= Do you speak French?
No, amigo, pero mi hermano lo habla muy bien	= No, friend, but my brother speaks it very well.
¿Habla inglés?	= Does he speak English?
No lo habla	= He doesn't speak it.
¿Por qué no?	= Why not?
Porque no lo sabe	= Because he doesn't know it.
¿Dónde está el libro?	= Where is the book?
Está en el cuarto	= It is in the room.
Sí, pero ¿en qué cuarto?	= Yes, but in which room?
En el cuarto de mi hijo	= In my son's room.
¿Cómo se llama aquella señora?	= What is that lady's name?
Se llama la señora de Romanos	= She is called Mrs. Romanos.
¿Qué tiene en la mano?	= What has she in her hand?
Tiene un periódico español	= She has a Spanish newspaper.
¿Habla ella español?	= Does she speak Spanish?
Ella habla no solamente español sino también inglés	= She speaks not only Spanish but also English.
¿Es bueno este libro?	= Is this book good?
Sí, caballero, es muy bueno	= Yes, sir, it is very good.
¿Es buena esta naranja?	= Is this orange good?
No, amigo, es mala	= No, friend, it is bad.
¿Quién tiene mi lápiz?	= Who has my pencil?

Mi primo lo tiene	= My cousin has it.
¿De quién es esta flor?	= Whose (of whom) is this flower?
Es de mi prima	= It is my cousin's (*fem.*).
¿Está el soldado en casa?	= Is the soldier at home?
No, señor, no está en casa	= No, sir, he is not at home.
¿Dónde está?	= Where is he?
No sé, señor	= I don't know, sir.
¿Por qué no lo sabe Vd.?	= Why don't you know?
Porque no me gusta ese soldado	= Because I don't like that soldier.
¡Adiós!	= Good-bye!

Notes

The student will undoubtedly have remarked a few peculiarities in the foregoing exercise which will have led him to seek an explanation of them.

(1) The various parts of a verb may be used without the pronoun, customary in English. Hence the Spaniard will say **es** for 'he is' or 'she is' or 'it is' or 'you are' (with **Vd.**).

(2) Some words precede the verb in Spanish where they follow it in English, as in **No lo sé** signifying 'I don't know.' Here **lo** (*it*) precedes the verb **sé**. This order of words in the sentence must be closely studied by the beginner, for it bears greatly upon both clear understanding and intelligible expression. We shall notice the same point later with respect to adjectives and the nouns they qualify.

(3) **De** signifies 'of'. Since it has a possessive signification, it becomes equivalent to the English ''s', so that **de mi padre** may be translated into English either 'of my father' or 'my father's'.

(4) Notice the difference between **esta** (without an accent) signifying 'this', and **está** (with an accent) signifying 'is'.

(5) It should be observed that Spanish adjectives agree, both in gender and number, with the nouns they accompany. The adjective 'good' used with a masculine singular noun is

therefore **bueno**, with a feminine singular noun **buena**, with the plurals **buenos** and **buenas** according to gender.

(6) In order to make a sentence interrogative the verb precedes the pronoun. There is, in such cases, no Spanish equivalent for our interrogative 'do?' and 'does?'

(7) Take care over the pronunciation of words which are spelled alike yet differently accented; **esta** and **porque** are accented on the first syllable; **está** on the final syllable and **por qué** on the **qué**. To accentuate wrongly is to be misunderstood, of course.

IV

THE SECOND LESSON

THE student ought on no account to commence the study of this lesson until he has mastered every rule and Spanish word and sentence in the previous chapter. By employing those odd moments, precious enough, which occur throughout the day in a careful revision and repetition of them, he will discover that language-learning is not so difficult as is popularly imagined, nor so irksome.

The possessive adjectives in Spanish are:

English	Singular	Plural
my	mi	mis
your	tu	tus
your	su	sus
his (her, its)	su	sus
our	nuestro, -a	nuestros, -as
your	vuestro, -a	vuestros, -as
your	su	sus
their	su	sus

mi casa	= my house
su amigo	= his (your, her, their) friend
nuestras vacaciones	= our holiday

Note that, just as there are different pronouns for 'you', depending on the degree of familiarity, there are corresponding possessive adjectives. The following examples should clarify their use:

tú has olvidado tu paraguas = you (familiar) have forgotten your umbrella

Vd. invita a sus amigos = you invite your friends

vosotros perdéis vuestro dinero = you (familiar) lose your money

Vds. visitan a su padre = you visit your father

22

The meaning of **su** and **sus** will usually be clear from the context, but it is necessary to use a different expression when ambiguity arises:

la madre de Vd. tiene más dinero que la tía de él = your mother has more money than his aunt

The possessive pronouns are:

mine	**mío, -a**	**míos, -as**
yours	**tuyo, -a**	**tuyos, -as**
yours	**suyo, -a**	**suyos, -as**
his (her, its)	**suyo, -a**	**suyos, -as**
ours	**nuestro, -a**	**nuestros, -as**
yours	**vuestro, -a**	**vuestros, -as**
yours	**suyo, -a**	**suyos, -as**
theirs	**suyo, -a**	**suyos, -as**

tu amigo y el mío = your friend and mine
nuestra casa es más grande que la suya = our house is bigger than his (yours, theirs, hers)

The appropriate definite article is required except when the possessive pronoun is the complement of **ser**:

aquel coche es mío = that car is mine

Note also the following construction:

un amigo mío   = a friend of mine
unos amigos suyos = some friends of his (yours, theirs, hers)

Like **su, el suyo** can be ambiguous, in which case an expression such as the following must be used:

nuestro jardín es más grande que el de Vd. = our garden is bigger than yours
este sombrero es de ella = this hat is hers

There are three conjugations of verbs, their infinitives ending respectively in **-ar, -er,** and **-ir.**

Their present indicative tenses are as follows:

hablar (to speak, talk)	*temer* (to fear)	*permitir* (to permit)
yo hablo	temo	permito
tú hablas	temes	permites
Vd. habla	teme	permite
él habla	teme	permite
nosotros hablamos	tememos	permitimos
vosotros habláis	teméis	permitís
Vds. hablan	temen	permiten
ellos hablan	temen	permiten

The personal pronouns are:

	Subject	Direct Object	Indirect Object
I	yo	me	me
you (*fam.*)	tú	te	te
you	usted	le, la	le
he, it	él	le, lo	le
she, it	ella	la	le
it (*neuter*)	ello	lo	le
we	nosotros, -as	nos	nos
you (*fam.*)	vosotros, -as	os	os
you	ustedes	los, las	les
they (*masc.*)	ellos	los	les
they (*fem.*)	ellas	las	les

The subject pronoun **ello** is rarely used, and is mainly confined to the expression **ello es que . . .** = 'the fact is that . . .'
'It' as a subject is not otherwise expressed in Spanish, thus:

it is raining	= **llueve** *or* **está lloviendo**
it is late	= **es tarde**
it is dead (of an animal)	= **está muerto**

It will be noted that the direct object pronoun for 'him' is either **le** or **lo**. Both are commonly used in Spain, though perhaps it is preferable to use **le** for 'him' and **lo** for 'it'. In South America **lo** is widely used for 'him' and 'it'.

The position of object pronouns is before the verb, unless the verb is an infinitive, affirmative imperative, or *gerundio* (an explanation of the latter is given in the fourth lesson):

mi padre me da dinero = my father gives me some money
alguien nos mira   = somebody is watching us
lo vendo a mi amigo   = I sell it to my friend
les damos agua   = we give them some water

When it is necessary to distinguish between **le** meaning 'him' and **le** meaning 'you', **a él** and **a Vd.** are added:

le veo a Vd. pero no le veo a él = I see you, but I do not see him

Similarly, **le** meaning 'to him', 'to her', or 'to you' will be clarified by adding **a él, a ella,** or **a Vd.**

The student will have noticed that in the above example the preposition **a** precedes **Vd.** and **él**, although they are direct objects. The rule is that when a noun or pronoun representing a definite person is the direct object of a verb, it is preceded by **a**. The following examples further illustrate the point:

voy a ver al médico = I am going to see the doctor
seguimos a Juan hasta la puerta = we follow Juan as far as the door
no veo a nadie = I do not see anybody
¿A quién mira Vd.? = Who are you looking at?

To return to object pronouns, if both a direct and an indirect object are required the indirect object always comes first, and if both objects are in the third person the indirect **le** or **les** changes to **se**.

me lo da   = he gives it to me
nos los dan   = they give them to us
se lo doy   = I give it to him (to you, to her)
se los damos a Vds. = we give them to you

After prepositions the personal pronouns used are as follows:

me	= **mí**	it	= **ello**
you	= **ti**	us	= **nosotros, -as**
you	= **Vd.**	you	= **vosotros, -as**
him	= **él**	you	= **Vds.**
her	= **ella**	them	= **ellos, ellas**

lo compro para él = I buy it for him
está delante de nosotros = it is in front of us
no hay nada para Vds. = there is nothing for you

There is an additional form **sí** which means 'himself', 'herself', 'yourself', 'themselves', 'yourselves'.

lo compra para sí = he buys it for himself
Vds. los compran para sí = you buy them for yourselves

With the preposition **con** there are three special forms of pronoun:

yo lo traigo conmigo = I bring it with me
tú lo traes contigo = you bring it with you
él lo trae consigo = he brings it with him
ellas los traen consigo = they bring them with them

Note the use of the verb **gustar.** It means literally 'to please', but is the usual word for 'to like', used as follows:

me gusta el vino = I like wine
nos gusta ir al cine = we like going to the cinema
les gustan los plátanos = they like bananas
a Juan no le gusta esta película = Juan does not like this film

The degrees of comparison of adjectives are formed thus:

feliz = happy
más feliz que —— = happier than ——
tan feliz como —— = as happy as ——
menos feliz que —— = less happy than ——

The superlatives are formed thus:

el más feliz = the happiest
el menos feliz = the least happy

Study carefully the following irregularities:

	Positive.	*Comparative.*	*Superlative.*
good	**bueno**	**mejor**	**el mejor**
bad	**malo**	**peor**	**el peor**
large	**grande**	**mayor**	**el mayor**
small	**pequeño**	**menor**	**el menor**

With **grande** and **pequeño** the regular comparatives and superlatives with **más** are used when these adjectives refer to size rather than importance. Note also the following:

mi hermano mayor = my eldest brother
su hermana menor = his younger sister
es mayor que yo = he is older than me

VOCABULARY

voy	= I go	**caro**	= dear
vas	= you go	**alto, a**	= high, tall
va	= he goes	**para**	= for
vamos	= we go	**guapo, a**	= pretty
vais	= you go	**la lengua**	= language
van	= they go	**hacer**	= to make, do
ahí	= there	**el frío**	= cold (coldness)
la mano	= hand	**la ciudad**	= town
el reloj	= watch	**tal vez**	= perhaps, maybe
la botella	= bottle	**aprender**	= to learn
poco, poca	= little	**¿quiere Vd.?**	= do you want, wish, love?
siento	= I feel (I am sorry)	**querer**	= to want, wish, love
la plata	= silver		
puede	= he (it, she) can	**la cosa**	= thing
tener sed	= to be thirsty	**o —— o**	= either —— or
el vino	= wine	**ni —— ni**	= neither ——nor
vende	= he sells	**cuando**	= when
costar	= to cost	**la mañana**	= morning
cuesta	= it costs	**tomar**	= to take

un pedazo	= piece, bit	el idioma	= language
el jardín	= garden	bastante	= enough
con	= with	hace	= does, makes
sobre	= on	el calor	= heat
la mantequilla	= butter	estudiar	= to study
por	= by, for	el tiempo	= time; weather
desear	= to wish, desire	quiero	= I want, wish, love
la pronunciación	= pronunciation		
la semana	= week	entonces	= then
escribir	= to write	la cerveza	= beer
la carta	= letter	la vez	= time (ordinal)
la caja	= box	dos veces	= twice
triste	= sad	de vez en cuando	= from time to time
fácil	= easy		
joven	= young	el café	= coffee
poder	= to be able (can)	dar	= to give
Vd. puede	= you can	doy	= I give
¡dispense Vd.!	= pardon!	das	= you give
recibir	= to receive	da	= he gives
vengo	= I come	damos	= we give
vienes	= you come	dais	= you give
viene	= he comes	dan	= they give
venimos	= we come	aquí	= here
venís	= you come	conmigo	= with me
vienen	= they come	la mesa	= table
trabaja	= he works	el favor	= favour, kindness
quiero	= I want		
quiere	= he wants	el placer	= pleasure
el agua	= water	pronunciar	= to pronounce
hay	= there is, there are	mandar	= to send
		algo	= anything, something
pocos, pocas	= few		
el oro	= gold	el cuchillo	= knife
enfermo	= ill	feliz	= happy
tener hambre	= to be hungry	difícil	= difficult
el vaso	= glass	viejo	= old
vender	= to sell	puedo	= I can
barato	= cheap	pueden	= they can
otro, a	= other, another	el paquete	= parcel
gordo, a	= fat, stout	allí, ahí	= there
el mes	= month		

CONVERSATIONAL MATTER

¿De dónde vienen Vds., señores?	= Where do you come from, gentlemen?
Venimos del teatro	= We come from the theatre.
¿Quién está ahí?	= Who is there?
Mi padre está ahí	= My father is there.
¿Qué quiere Vd.?	= What do you want?
No quiero nada	= I want nothing.
¿Qué quiere este hombre?	= What does this man want?
Creo que quiere dinero	= I believe (think) he wants money.
¿Por qué quiere dinero?	= Why does he want money?
Porque es un hombre muy pobre	= Because he is a very poor man.
¿Por qué es pobre?	= Why is he poor?
Porque no trabaja	= Because he doesn't work.
¿Por qué no trabaja?	= Why doesn't he work?
Porque es perezoso	= Because he is lazy.
¿Por qué es perezoso?	= Why is he lazy?
Porque no quiere trabajar	= Because he doesn't want to work.
¿Es perezoso también su padre?	= Is his father also lazy?
Sí, es perezoso	= Yes, he is lazy.
¿Es perezosa también su madre?	= Is his mother also lazy?
Sí, pero no tan perezosa como su padre	= Yes, but not so lazy as his father.
¿Qué tiene Vd. en la mano?	= What have you in your hand?
No tengo nada en la mano derecha	= I have nothing in my right hand.
¿Pero qué tiene Vd. en la mano izquierda?	= But what have you in your left hand?
Tengo mi reloj	= I have my watch.
¿Hay agua en la botella?	= Is there any water in the bottle?
Creo que hay muy poca	= I think (believe) there is very little.
No hay vino en esta botella	= There is no wine in this bottle.
Lo siento mucho	= I am very sorry.

¿Es de oro o de plata este reloj? = Is this watch gold or silver?

No sé, pero creo que es de plata = I don't know, but I think it is silver.

¿Está Vd. enfermo? = Are you ill?

No, amigo, no estoy enfermo = No, friend, I'm not ill.

¿Tiene hambre su amigo de Vd.? = Is your friend hungry?

¡Puede ser! = It may be! (Perhaps.)

¿Tiene sed también? = Is he thirsty also?

No lo creo = I don't think so.

¿Quiere Vd. un vaso de vino? = Do you want a glass of wine?

Sí, señor, por favor = Yes, sir, please.

¿Tiene este alumno muchos amigos? = Has this pupil many friends?

No tiene muchos = He hasn't many.

¿No hay leche? = Is there no milk?

No, señora, no la hay = No, madam, there isn't any.

¿Vende Vd. periódicos ingleses? = Do you sell English newspapers?

Sí, señor, los vendo = Yes, sir, I sell them.

¿Cuánto cuesta este libro? = How much does this book cost?

No cuesta mucho; es muy barato = It doesn't cost much; it's very cheap.

¿Es caro éste? [1] = Is this one dear?

No tan caro como el otro = Not so dear as the other.

Mi hermano es más alto que mi padre = My brother is taller than my father.

¿Es verdad? = Is that so (Is it true?)

Sí, pero mi hermana no es tan alta como mi madre = Yes, but my sister is not so tall as my mother.

¿Y su tío? = And your uncle?

Es muy gordo = He is very stout (fat).

¿Y su tía también? = And your aunt, too?

O, no, señor, ella no es tan gorda como él = Oh, no, sir, she isn't so fat as he is.

[1] The demonstrative pronoun is pronounced as the adjective, but has a written accent on the stressed vowel.

¿Es para mí la carta?	= Is the letter for me?
No, señorita, es para mí	= No, miss, it is for me.
¿Cuántos meses tiene el año?	= How many months has the year?
El año tiene doce meses	= The year has twelve months.
¿Adónde va Vd.?	= Where are you going?
Voy al teatro	= I am going to the theatre.
¿Con quién?	= With whom?
Con mis hermanas	= With my sisters.
¿Son guapas?	= Are they pretty?
Sí, son muy guapas	= Yes, they are very pretty.
¿Dónde están sus hijos de Vd.?	= Where are your sons?
Están en Londres	= They are in London.
¿Qué hace su hija de él?	= What does his daughter do?
No sé qué hace	= I don't know what she does.
¿Qué idioma habla?	= What language does she speak?
Habla francés bastante bien	= She speaks French quite well.
¿No habla ella otra lengua?	= Doesn't she speak any other language?
Creo que no	= I don't think so.
¿Hace frío, hoy?	= Is it cold today?
No, señor, hace mucho calor	= No, sir, it is very hot.
¿Va Vd. a la ciudad?	= Are you going to town?
Creo que no; hace demasiado frío	= I don't think so; it is too cold.
¿No le gusta el frío?	= Don't you like the cold?
No me gusta	= I don't like it.
¿Le gusta el calor, tal vez?	= You like the heat, perhaps?
¡Eso, sí!	= That, yes!
¿Habla Vd. italiano?	= Do you speak Italian?
Lo hablo un poco, pero no mucho	= I speak it a little, but not much.
¿Estudia Vd. otro idioma?	= Are you studying any other language?
No, señora, no tengo suficiente tiempo	= No, madam, I have not enough time.
Tal vez trabaja Vd. mucho	= Perhaps you work a lot.

Sí, trabajo todo el día	= Yes, I work all day.
¿Qué quiere Vd. comer?	= What do you want to eat?
No quiero comer nada	= I don't wish to eat anything.
¿Qué quiere ella beber?	= What does she want to drink?
Quiere un vaso de vino	= She wants a glass of wine.
Pero no tengo vino	= But I have no wine.
¡Qué lástima! ¿Tiene Vd. otra cosa?	= What a pity! Have you anything else?
Sí, tengo dos botellas de cerveza	= Yes, I have two bottles of beer.
No le gusta a ella la cerveza	= She doesn't like beer.
¿Qué bebe ella, pues?	= What does she drink, then?
Bebe vino o agua	= She drinks wine or water.
Yo no bebo ni vino ni agua	= I drink neither wine nor water.
¿Qué bebe Vd., pues?	= What do you drink, then?
Bebo una taza de té de vez en cuando	= I drink a cup of tea from time to time.
¿Nada más?	= Nothing more?
Es decir que, por la mañana, tomo una taza de café de vez en cuando	= That's to say, that, in the morning, I take a cup of coffee from time to time.
No hay ningún periódico en el cuarto de Vd.	= There is no newspaper in your room.
¿Dónde está, pues?	= Where is it, then?
Está en el jardín	= It is in the garden.
¿Quiere Vd. venir conmigo?	= Do you wish to come with me?
Sí, señor, lo quiero	= Yes, I wish to, sir.
¿Es Vd. inglés?	= Are you English?
Sí, señor, lo soy	= Yes, sir, I am.
Vd. habla español muy bien	= You speak Spanish very well.
¿Es verdad?	= Is that so? (true?)
Sí, su pronunciación es muy buena	= Yes, your pronunciation is very good.
¿Cómo se pronuncia esta palabra, por favor?	= How is this word pronounced, please?
Se pronuncia así ——	= It is pronounced like this.
¿Escribe Vd. muchas cartas?	= Do you write many letters?

No muchas, porque no tengo = Not many, because I haven't
 muchos amigos   many friends.
¿Dónde están nuestros cuchillos? = Where are our knives?
Están en esta caja   = They are in this box.
¿Y dónde están los tenedores de = And where are your forks?
 Vd.?
Están también allí   = They are also there.
¿Está Vd. contento?   = Are you happy?
No, amigo, estoy muy triste   = No, friend, I'm very sad.
¿Por qué está Vd. triste?   = Why are you sad?
Porque no hablo español bien   = Because I do not speak Spanish
         well.
¿Están Vds. contentos?   = Are you happy?
Sí, señor, estamos contentos   = Yes, sir, we are happy.
¿Cuántos días tiene una semana? = How many days has a week?
Una semana tiene siete días   = A week has seven days.
¿Es difícil esta lección?   = Is this lesson difficult?
No, es muy fácil   = No, it is very easy.
¿Es joven aquel inglés?   = Is that Englishman young?
No, es muy viejo   = No, he is very old.
Creo que no es tan viejo como mi = I don't believe he is as old as
 padre   my father.
¿Puede Vd. decirme quién tiene = Can you tell me who has my
 mi sombrero?   hat?
Dispense Vd.; yo lo tengo   = Pardon; I've got it.
¿Tienen Vds. bastante pan?   = Have you enough bread?
Sí, señores, tenemos bastante   = Yes, gentlemen, we have
         enough.
¿Para quién es este paquete? = For whom is this parcel?
Es para mi primo   = It's for my cousin.
Me gusta mucho recibir paquetes = I like to receive parcels very
         much.
A mí también   = So do I.

Notes

All the sentences in the 'Conversational Matter' are intended to be read aloud, over and over again, with their necessary 'tone' and 'expression', just as though a real conversation were taking place. Reading aloud is the best of all methods to adopt in order that one may become fluent. It is also, with reference to language-study, of wonderful assistance to the memory. Should the student desire written exercises as tests, he can employ the 'Conversational Matter' for this purpose. Dozens of other sentences can also be formed by substituting other words.

V

THE THIRD LESSON

EXPRESSING commands needs special care in Spanish, since there is one form for use with **tú** and **vosotros**, the imperative mood, while for other pronouns a different form, the present subjunctive, is used. When consulting a verb table, the student should always remember that the forms given under the heading 'Imperative' apply only to **tú** and **vosotros**. If he wants to find the command forms for **usted** and **ustedes** he must look under the heading 'Present Subjunctive'. Moreover, the imperative proper is limited to positive commands, and even with **tú** and **vosotros** the present subjunctive must be used in negative commands.

The forms of command for regular verbs are as follows:

	hablar	*temer*	*permitir*
(tú)	habla	teme	permite
(vosotros)	hablad	temed	permitid
(Vd.)	hable	tema	permita
(nosotros)	hablemos	temamos	permitamos
(Vds.)	hablen	teman	permitan

Some of the more common irregular verbs form their imperatives thus:

	tener	*ser*	*estar*	*mostrar*	*poner*	*traer*	*dormir*
(tú)	ten	sé	estate	muestra	pon	trae	duerme
(Vd.)	tenga	sea	esté	muestre	ponga	traiga	duerma

	pedir	*venir*	*ir*	*decir*	*hacer*	*salir*	*dar*
(tú)	pide	ven	ve	di	haz	sal	da
(Vd.)	pida	venga	vaya	diga	haga	salga	dé

Remember that pronoun objects follow affirmative imperatives but precede negative imperatives:

> **muéstreme Vd. su álbum** = show me your album
> **muéstremelo Vd.** = show it to me
> **no me pida Vd. dinero** = do not ask me for money

35

no me lo pida Vd. = do not ask me for it
dime tu nombre = tell me your name
no me digas mentiras = do not tell me lies

Notice that when pronoun objects are added to an imperative it is necessary to place a written accent on the verb in order to preserve the same stress as when the verb is used without an object.

Some consideration must now be given to negatives. The more usual expressions are as follows:

no	= no; not	**ni ... ni ...**	= neither ... nor ...
nada	= nothing	**ninguno, -a**	= no; none
nadie	= nobody	**en ninguna parte**	= nowhere
nunca	= never	**tampoco**	= neither
jamás	= never; ever		

When they are placed after the verb **no** must precede the verb:

nadie viene *or* **no viene nadie** = nobody is coming
nunca llega tarde *or* **no llega nunca tarde** = he never arrives late

The demonstrative adjectives are as follows:

	Masculine	*Feminine*
this	**este**	**esta**
these	**estos**	**estas**
that	**ese**	**esa**
	aquel	**aquella**
those	**esos**	**esas**
	aquellos	**aquellas**

The distinction between **ese** and **aquel** is that **ese** refers to a thing near the person being addressed, and **aquel** refers to a thing some distance away, thus:

tráigame ese libro = bring me that book (near you)
tráigame aquel libro = bring me that book (yonder)

The demonstrative pronouns are the same as the adjectives, but they have a written accent on the stressed vowel:

prefiero este libro a aquél = I prefer this book to that (one)
aquella casa no es tan grande como ésta = that house is not as big as this (one)

There are also neuter pronouns, used to refer to things to which a gender cannot be given:

¿qué es esto?	= what is this?
no me gusta eso	= I do not like that
aquello fue lo que dijo	= that was what he said

Note that **éste**, etc., also means 'the latter' and that **aquél**, etc., also means 'the former'.

VOCABULARY

subir	= to go up; take up	en seguida	= immediately
prestar	= to lend	el lápiz	= pencil
buscar	= to look for	la leña	= firewood
el país	= country (e.g. Spain)	el campo	= country (not town)
el fuego	= fire	el baúl	= trunk, box
el rincón	= corner	ahora	= now
la guerra	= war	la llave	= key
el comedor	= dining-room	limpiar	= to clean
cerrar	= to shut	ayudar	= to help
encender	= to light	la lámpara	= lamp
dejar	= to leave	la carne	= meat
por favor	= (if you) please	creer	= to believe
tomar	= to take	costar	= to cost

CONVERSATIONAL MATTER

Tráigame Vd. un vaso de vino	= Bring me a glass of wine.
Lleve Vd. mi equipaje a la casa	= Take my luggage to the house.
Vaya Vd. a mi cuarto	= Go into my room.
Suba Vd. a mi cuarto	= Go up to my room.
Vamos en seguida	= Let us go at once.
Indíqueme Vd. la casa del Señor González	= Show me Mr. Gonzalez' house.
Tenga Vd. la bondad de ——	= Please be good enough to ——
Déme Vd. un pedazo de pan	= Give me a piece of bread.
Muéstreme Vd. el periódico	= Show me the newspaper.
Présteme unos lápices	= Lend me a few (some) pencils.
Aquí está uno, señor	= Here is one, sir.
Muchas gracias	= Many thanks.

Tengamos paciencia	= Let us be patient.
Búsquelo	= Look for it.
Llévelas Vd.	= Take them. (Carry them.)
Condúzcame Vd. a este punto	= Conduct me to this point (place).
Entremos	= Let us go in.
Súbame Vd. un poco de leña	= Bring me up a little wood.
Dígame Vd. su nombre	= Tell me your name.
Hábleme Vd. de su país	= Tell me about your country.
Ponga Vd. mi baúl en el rincón	= Put my trunk in the corner.
Hablemos ahora de la guerra	= Let us talk now about (of) the war.
Enséñeme Vd. en donde se encuentra la llave	= Show me where the key is.
Vamos ahora al comedor	= Let us go now into the dining-room.
Vayan Vds. a la iglesia	= Go (plur.) to church.
Limpie Vd. esta taza	= Clean this cup.
¡Oiga Vd.!	= Listen! I say!
¡Oígame Vd.!	= Listen to me!
¡Oígale Vd.!	= Listen to him!
¡Cuidado!	= Take care!
Cierre Vd. la puerta	= Shut the door.
Cierre Vd. la ventana	= Shut the window.
Ayúdeme Vd. a subir	= Help me to climb up.
Encienda Vd. la lámpara	= Light the lamp.
No deje Vd. nada en la mesa	= Leave nothing on the table.
Páseme Vd. el azúcar	= Pass me the sugar.
Páseme Vd. la sal	= Pass me the salt.
Páseme Vd. la carne, por favor	= Pass me the meat, please.
Dénos Vd. patatas	= Give us some potatoes.
¿Habla Vd. inglés?	= Do you speak English?
Hable Vd. español	= Speak Spanish.
Dispense Vd.	= Excuse me.
Créame Vd. Don Pedro, no tengo nada	= Believe me, Don Pedro, I have nothing.
¿Qué hora es?	= What time is it?
¿Qué hora tiene Vd.?	= What time do you make it?

Dígame Vd. qué hora es	= Tell me what time it is.
Es la una	= It is one o'clock.
Son las cinco	= It is five o'clock.
Son las ocho y media	= It is half-past eight.
Son las nueve y cuarto	= It is a quarter-past nine.
Son las seis menos veinte	= It is twenty to six.
Dígame Vd. si es tarde	= Tell me if it is late.
Con mucho gusto, señor; no es tarde; al contrario es muy temprano	= With much pleasure, sir; it's not late; on the contrary, it's very early.
Esté Vd. persuadido que es así, señor	= Be certain that it is so, sir.
¿Quién tiene mi libro?	= Who has my book?
Yo lo tengo	= I have it.
¿Qué tiene Vd.?	= What have you?
Tengo la flor que Vd. me ha dado	= I have the flower which you have given me.
¿Cómo se llama Vd.?	= What is your name?
Me llamo Antonio	= I am called Antonio.
Aquí está el muchacho cuyo padre ha muerto	= Here is the boy whose father has died.
¿De quién es este caballo?	= Whose horse is this?
Es el caballo de aquel soldado	= It is that soldier's horse.
Ponga Vd. una botella de vino en la mesa	= Put a bottle of wine on the table.
¿La quiere Vd. ahora?	= Do you want it now?
Sí, la quiero inmediatamente	= Yes, I want it immediately.
Camarero, tráigame otra cosa	= Waiter, bring me something else.
No tome Vd. esto	= Don't take this.
¿Qué hay?	= What is the matter?
¿Qué tiene Vd.?	= What is the matter with you?
Tráiganos Vd. la lista	= Bring us the menu.
Tráigame Vd. cerveza	= Bring me some beer.
¿Cuánto cuesta?	= How much does it cost?
¡Vamos!	= Let's go! Come on!
Vamos a ver	= Let's see.
Vamos al cine	= Let's go to the cinema.

Vamos a comer	= Let's go and eat.
Vamos a estudiar esta lección	= Let's study this lesson.
¿Me hace el favor de decirme la hora?	= Will you please tell me the time?
¿Me hace el favor?	= Do you mind? Excuse me!
¿Quiere Vd. decirme dónde vive?	= Will you tell me where he lives?
No le veo nunca	= I never see him.
No le veo en ninguna parte	= I don't see him anywhere.
Nadie dice nada	= Nobody says anything.
Nunca dice nada	= He never says anything.
Se marcha sin decir nada	= He goes away without saying anything.
No viene nadie	= Nobody is coming.
¿De qué color es ese libro?	= What colour is that book?
Este libro es verde	= This book is green.
¿De quién es aquella casa?	= Whose is that house?
Aquella casa es del señor Martínez	= That house is Mr. Martinez'.
¿Qué es eso?	= What is that?
Esto es mi reloj	= This is my watch.

Now learn by heart the following lines, which are amusing, and may be repeated over and over again and still interest.

> Las dos de la noche eran
> Cuando sentí ruido en casa.
> Subo la escalera ansiosa;
> Saco la brillante espada.
> Toda la casa registro,
> Y en ella no encuentro nada.
> Y por ser cosa curiosa
> Voy a volver a contarla.[1]
> Las dos de la noche eran
> Cuando sentí ruido en casa, etc., etc.

[1] **Volver** signifies 'to turn, to return'; when used in conjunction with the infinitive of another verb it denotes repetition of that verb, viz., **volver a ver** (to see again).

Translation

Two o'clock in the night (it) was
When (I) heard a noise in (the) house.
(I) mount the staircase anxious;
(I) draw out the brilliant sword.
All the house (the whole house) I inspect,
And in it (I) meet nothing.
And for (its) being a curious thing
I am going to relate it to you again.[1]
Two o'clock, etc.

The student must be prepared to encounter all manner of suffixes to nouns, indicating or suggesting proportion both diminution and augmentation, love, contempt, tenderness, etc. These may be set under two headings, diminution and augmentation.

The feminine is formed by the addition of **a**.

The principal forms are:

Diminutives	*Augmentatives*
-ito	**-ón**
-ico	**-azo**
-itico	**-ote**
-illo	**-achón**
-uelo	**-acho**
-ucho	
-cito, ececito	
-zuelo, etc.	

Examples

perro	= dog	**perrón**	= big dog
capa	= cloak, cape	**capote**	= big cape
pie	= foot	**piececito**	= little foot
pueblo	= small town	**pueblecito**	= village
flor	= flower	**florecita**	= little flower
casa	= house	**casita**	= cottage; bungalow
mujer	= woman	**mujercita**	= little woman

From this point one repeats over again from the beginning.

This habitual use of diminutives and augmentatives by the Spanish has actually given birth to new words with often a changed meaning.

Note carefully the following:

Original Word	*Derived Word*
puño = fist	**puñetazo** = a punch, a blow with the fist
paño = cloth	**pañuelo** = handkerchief
cera = wax	**cerilla** = match (for lighting)
palo = stick	**palillo** = small stick, or toothpick

Proper names may also receive these suffixes, often suggestive of affection.

Juan (John) becomes **Juanito**
Luisa (Louise) becomes **Luisita**

VI

THE FOURTH LESSON

THE perfect tense is formed with the present indicative of **haber** and the past participle of the verb in question. Past participles of regular verbs are as follows:

> **hablar**   **hablado** (spoken)
> **temer**   **temido** (feared)
> **permitir** **permitido** (permitted)

> **he hablado**   = I have spoken
> **Vd. ha temido**   = you have feared
> **hemos permitido** = we have permitted

Here are the more common irregular past participles:

escribir (to write)	**escrito**	**poner** (to put)	**puesto**
abrir (to open)	**abierto**	**volver** (to return)	**vuelto**
cubrir (to cover)	**cubierto**	**ver** (to see)	**visto**
morir (to die)	**muerto**	**imprimir** (to print)	**impreso**
hacer (to do, make)	**hecho**	**resolver** (to solve,	
decir (to say)	**dicho**	resolve)	**resuelto**

The student who knows French should be particularly careful about the use of the perfect tense. In Spanish it is not used automatically in conversation, but corresponds more nearly to the use of the perfect in English. The usual Spanish equivalent of the French perfect is the preterite tense, which is dealt with in a later chapter.

Other compound tenses than the perfect are formed in the same way as the perfect. The future perfect is formed with the future of **haber** and the past participle, the pluperfect with the imperfect of **haber** and the past participle.

Note that the past participle is the verbal adjective in Spanish, and study the following examples:

> **estamos sentados en el jardín** = we are sitting in the garden
> **el cuadro está colgado en la pared** = the picture is hanging on the wall
> **está tendido en la cama** = he is lying on the bed

Being used as an adjective, the participle in these examples agrees in number and gender with the subject, but when it is used with **haber** to form compound tenses the participle is invariable:

> **nos hemos sentado en el jardín** = we have sat down in the garden
> **los han colgado en la pared** = they have hung them on the wall

The 'gerundio' is a part of the verb which appears to correspond to the English present participle, but great care must be taken in using it. It cannot be used as a noun or as an adjective, and the examples given below should be carefully noted. It is formed as follows:

hablar	**hablando** (speaking)
temer	**temiendo** (fearing)
permitir	**permitiendo** (permitting)

The more common irregular forms are:

sentir (to feel)	**sintiendo**	**decir** (to say)	**diciendo**
dormir (to sleep)	**durmiendo**	**venir** (to come)	**viniendo**
pedir (to ask for)	**pidiendo**	**traer** (to bring)	**trayendo**
morir (to die)	**muriendo**	**poder** (to be able)	**pudiendo**
ir (to go)	**yendo**		

Examples

estoy leyendo una revista	= I am reading a magazine
están durmiendo la siesta	= they are having a siesta
va corriendo a su padre	= he is running to his father
salen corriendo a la calle	= they run out into the street
bajan corriendo la escalera	= they run downstairs

andando por la calle, vi un acci-dente	= walking along the street I saw an accident
viéndole acercarse, me volví	= seeing him approach, I turned round
se gana la vida vendiendo perió-dicos	= he earns his living selling newspapers
siguen escribiéndoles	= they continue to write to them

It will be noted that the 'gerundio' is invariable, and that, as with the infinitive and the positive imperative, object pronouns follow it and are attached to it.

The Future Tense

hablar	*temer*	*permitir*
hablaré	**temeré**	**permitiré**
hablarás	**temerás**	**permitirás**
hablará	**temerá**	**permitirá**
hablaremos	**temeremos**	**permitiremos**
hablaréis	**temeréis**	**permitiréis**
hablarán	**temerán**	**permitirán**

The future endings are the same for all verbs, and in the following list of verbs which form their future irregularly only the first person singular is given.

tener (to have)	**tendré**	**decir** (to say)	**diré**
haber (to have)	**habré**	**hacer** (to do, make)	**haré**
saber (to know)	**sabré**	**venir** (to come)	**vendré**
querer (to want, love)	**querré**	**salir** (to go out)	**saldré**
poner (to put)	**pondré**	**poder** (to be able)	**podré**

The student must always be prepared for slight changes in the forms of some verbs. Although the changes are, in most cases, so slight that the word may be recognized in the text, it is essential that the beginner should become familiar with them in order to be able to employ them readily in conversation. However simple a word may appear, as much care must be taken in learning it as over any difficult one.

These changes in the form of certain parts only of the verb will be found to be quite reasonable, as the following examples will show.

The main point to be remembered is that the final consonant sound of the stem of a verb must not change, whatever is added to it as a suffix.

Tocar means 'to touch', and the stem is **toc**.

This 'c' sound (as in 'cat') must remain throughout the conjugation. In the present we have **toco**, meaning 'I touch'.

Now, in order to form the 'past definite' (I touched) we must add suffix **-é**, but if this vowel follows **c**, 'c's' sound is changed, and it becomes equivalent to English 'th'. This must not be, so we substitute **qu** for the **c** and the stem-consonant retains its phonetic value. The word now becomes **toqué** (I touched). Practice will soon show the student where these euphonic changes become necessary.

As with **c**, so with **g**.

Pagar means 'to pay'. The present is **pago**, the 'past definite' **pagué**.

Verbs which end in **-cer** and **-cir** in the infinitive have another change. The **c** becomes **z** before **a** and **o**. Note the present indicative of the verb **vencer** (to vanquish):

venzo	= I vanquish
vences	= you vanquish
vence	= he vanquishes
vencemos	= we vanquish
vencéis	= you vanquish
vencen	= they vanquish

Here the consonant-sound preceding the suffix is the same throughout.

The same rule must be noted in respect to verbs in **-ger**. Since this **g** is guttural, what will happen when the suffix is **o**? Some sound which is guttural before **o** must be substituted, since **go** is pronounced almost as in English. Here, then, we write and pronounce **jo**.

Coger means 'to gather'. The present indicative is:

cojo	= I gather
coges	= you gather
coge	= he gathers
cogemos	= we gather
cogéis	= you gather
cogen	= they gather

The first person of the present indicative of the verb **distinguir** is:

distingo = I distinguish

The remaining forms retain the 'u' after 'g'.

So with verbs terminating in **-quir**. **Qu** becomes **c** before **a** and **o**.

Delinquir signifies 'to transgress, to offend'.

> **delinco**
> **delinques**
> **delinque**, etc.

The euphonic value of **c** followed by **o** is equal to that of **'qu'** followed by **e**.

Radical-changing Verbs

A number of verbs change their stem when the latter is the stressed syllable. They can be conveniently dealt with in groups according to their infinitive endings.

1. (*a*) **cerrar** (to close) (*b*) **contar** (to count, relate) (*c*) **jugar** (to play)

cierro	**cuento**	**juego**
cierras	**cuentas**	**juegas**
cierra	**cuenta**	**juega**
cerramos	**contamos**	**jugamos**
cerráis	**contáis**	**jugáis**
cierran	**cuentan**	**juegan**

Other common verbs like these are:

(a) **pensar** (to think), **acertar** (to succeed), **apretar** (to press), **atravesar** (to cross), **calentar** (to heat), **comenzar** (to begin), **confesar** (to confess), **empezar** (to begin), **negar** (to deny), **negarse** (to refuse), **sentarse** (to sit down).

(b) **acordarse** (to remember), **acostarse** (to lie down), **almorzar** (to have lunch), **colgar** (to hang), **costar** (to cost), **encontrar** (to meet, find), **mostrar** (to show), **probar** (to try), **rogar** (to ask), **sonar** (to sound), **soñar** (to dream), **volar** (to fly).

2.   (a) **perder** (to lose)   (b) **volver** (to return)

(a) perder (to lose)	(b) volver (to return)
pierdo	vuelvo
pierdes	vuelves
pierde	vuelve
perdemos	volvemos
perdéis	volvéis
pierden	vuelven

Like (a) are: **ascender** (to ascend), **defender** (to defend), **entender** (to understand).

Like (b) are: **doler** (to hurt), **llover** (to rain), **morder** (to bite), **mover** (to move), **resolver** (to solve), **torcer** (to twist, turn).

3. (a) **pedir** (to ask for)   (b) **sentir** (to feel)   (c) **dormir** (to sleep)

(a) pedir (to ask for)	(b) sentir (to feel)	(c) dormir (to sleep)
pido	siento	duermo
pides	sientes	duermes
pide	siente	duerme
pedimos	sentimos	dormimos
pedís	sentís	dormís
piden	sienten	duermen

Like (a) are: **conseguir** (to succeed in), **corregir** (to correct), **elegir** (to elect), **impedir** (to prevent), **medir** (to measure), **repetir** (to repeat), **seguir** (to follow, continue), **servir** (to serve), **vestir** (to dress).

Like (b) are: **consentir** (to consent), **divertir** (to amuse), **mentir** (to tell a lie), **preferir** (to prefer), **sugerir** (to suggest).

Like (c) is: **morir** (to die).

An important point to remember about these verbs is that

groups 1 and 2 change only in the present tense (indicative and subjunctive), while group 3 verbs change in the present (indicative and subjunctive), the 'gerundio', the preterite, and the imperfect subjunctive.

A few other irregular verbs are:

Present Tense

poder (to be able)	valer (to be worth)	decir (to say)
puedo	valgo	digo
puedes	vales	dices
puede	vale	dice
podemos	valemos	decimos
podéis	valéis	decís
pueden	valen	dicen

traer (to bring)	oir (to hear)	dar (to give)
traigo	oigo	doy
traes	oyes	das
trae	oye	da
traemos	oímos	damos
traéis	oís	dais
traen	oyen	dan

poner (to put, place)	querer (to wish, love)	saber (to know)
pongo	quiero	sé
pones	quieres	sabes
pone	quiere	sabe
ponemos	queremos	sabemos
ponéis	queréis	sabéis
ponen	quieren	saben

hacer (to do)	ver (to see)
hago	veo
haces	ves
hace	ve
hacemos	vemos
hacéis	veis
hacen	ven

Some verbs, let it be noted, change their **c** to **zc** in the present tense.

> **aducir** (to adduce) forms **aduzco**
> **conocer** (to know) forms **conozco**
> **parecer** (to appear) forms **parezco**

VOCABULARY

el caballo	= horse
la cerilla	= match
siempre	= always
nunca	= never
el ruso	= Russian (language and race)
la flor	= flower
la llave	= key
diligente	= diligent
saber	= to know (understand)
ahora	= now
¿de veras?	= really, is that true?
perder	= to lose
comprar	= to buy
todavía no	= not yet
la americana	= coat
¡vea Vd.!	= look, see!
el país	= country
más tarde	= later
voy	= I go, am going
¿cuál?	= what, which?
todo, -a, -os, -as	= all
el mundo	= world
la noche	= night
pensar	= to think
llegar	= to arrive
seguro	= sure
mañana por la tarde	= tomorrow evening
mañana por la mañana	= tomorrow morning
trae	= brings
poder	= to be able (can)
la pipa	= pipe
fumar	= to smoke
parecer	= to appear, seem
lindo	= pretty
pedir	= to ask
sorprender	= to surprise
conocer	= to know (to be acquainted with)
mañana	= tomorrow
la plata	= silver
hallar	= to find
la bolsa	= purse
la tarjeta postal	= postcard
necesitar	= to want, need
allá	= there, over there
el clima	= climate
hago	= I do, make
el momento	= moment
jugar	= to play
¿cuáles? (*plur.*)	= what, which?
la estilográfica	= fountain pen
medio, media	= half
anoche	= last night
piensa	= thinks
llegado	= arrived
valer	= to be worth (have value)
la mañana	= the morning
traer	= to bring
partir	= to part, depart
¿puede Vd.?	= can you?

CONVERSATIONAL MATTER

¿Cuándo tendrá Vd. dinero?	= When will you have money?
Mañana por la mañana	= Tomorrow morning.
¿Tendrá Vd. mucho?	= Will you have very much?
No mucho, pero bastante	= Not much, but enough.
Parece que su padre de Vd. tiene unos caballos	= It appears that your father has a few horses.
Sí, es verdad, tiene nueve	= Yes, it's true, he has nine.
¿Tiene Vd. cerillas?	= Have you any matches?
Sí, señor, tengo unas	= Yes, sir, I have a few.
Parece que Vd. no fuma en pipa	= It seems that you don't smoke a pipe.
Nunca fumo en pipa; fumo siempre cigarros	= I never smoke a pipe; I always smoke cigars.
Aquí está un buen [1] cigarro	= Here is a good cigar.
Lo fumaré esta tarde	= I'll smoke it this evening.
¿Está Vd. escribiendo una carta a su hijo?	= Are you writing a letter to your son?
No, señorita, estoy escribiendo una carta a mi madre; mañana escribiré otra carta a mi padre	= No, miss, I am writing a letter to my mother; tomorrow I shall write another letter to my father.
¿Qué lengua está Vd. hablando?	= What language are you speaking?
Estoy hablando ruso	= I am speaking Russian.
¿Es verdad lo que tú me dices?	= Is it true what you are telling me?
Yo te lo digo porque es verdad	= I tell you it because it is true.
¿Qué está haciendo ella?	= What is she doing?
Está hablando al francés	= She is speaking to the Frenchman.
¿Ha visto Vd. al oficial?	= Have you seen the officer?
Sí, le he visto en la calle	= Yes, I have seen (saw) him in the street.

[1] **Bueno** drops its final **o** before a masculine singular noun. Other similar adjectives are **malo** (bad), **alguno** (some), **ninguno** (none), **primero** (first), **tercero** (third). **Grande** becomes **gran** before any singular noun.

Haga Vd. el favor de darme mi llave = Please give me my key.

Con mucho gusto; aquí está = With much pleasure; here it is.

¿Qué hace Vd.? = What are you doing?

Estoy escribiendo a mi padre para pedirle un poco de dinero = I am writing to my father to ask him for a little money.

¿Estudia el señor B—— el español? = Is Mr. B—— studying Spanish?

El señor B——no tiene tiempo para estudiar ningún idioma = Mr. B—— has no time to study any language.

¿Por qué no? = Why not?

Porque no le gusta a él el trabajo = Because he doesn't like work.

¿Es perezoso? = Is he lazy?

Sí, es más perezoso que el amigo de su hermano de Vd. = Yes, he's lazier than your brother's friend.

Pero, hombre, él no es perezoso; trabaja diez horas y media al día = But, good heavens, he isn't lazy; he works ten and a half hours a day.

Eso me sorprende, porque no parece muy diligente = That surprises me, because he doesn't seem very diligent.

Al contrario, es muy diligente; conoce muchos idiomas = On the contrary, he is very diligent; he knows many languages.

¿Dónde estará Vd. mañana? = Where will you be tomorrow?

Estaré o en mi cuarto o en el jardín; ¿por qué me pregunta Vd.? = I shall be either in my room or in the garden; why do you ask me?

Porque quiero saber, no más = Because I wish to know, that's all.

Pero, dígame, ¿por qué quiere Vd. saber? = But, tell me, why do you wish to know?

¿Es de oro su reloj de Vd.? = Is your watch gold?

No es más que de plata pero va muy bien = It is nothing more than silver, but it goes very well.

¿Ha leído Vd. el libro que le he dado? = Have you read the book that I have given (gave) to you?

Todavía no, pero lo leeré mañana, porque hoy no tengo tiempo	= Not yet, but I shall read it tomorrow, because I haven't enough time today.
¿Qué tiempo hace?	= What is the weather like?
Creo que llueve un poco	= I think it's raining a little.
¿Ha perdido Vd. algo?	= Have you lost something?
Sí, he perdido mi portamonedas	= Yes, I've lost my purse.
Lo he hallado	= I have found it.
¿Qué se ha comprado Vd.?	= What have you bought yourself?
Me he comprado una tarjeta postal	= I have bought myself a postcard.
¿Qué necesita Vd., señor?	= What do you want, sir?
Necesito un cuchillo para cortar este pan [1]	= I need a knife to cut this bread.
¿Necesita algo esta muchacha?	= Does this girl want anything?
Dice que necesita un alfiler	= She says she needs a pin.
Y este joven, ¿qué necesita?	= And this youth, what does he want?
No lo dice	= He doesn't say.
Pregúntele, por favor	= Ask him, please.
Dice que ha perdido su americana	= He says that he has lost his coat.
Piensa tal vez que yo la tengo	= He thinks perhaps that I have it.
Dice que la ha visto en su cuarto de Vd.	= He says he has seen it in your room.
No es verdad; vea Vd., está allá	= It's not true; see, it's over there.
¿Quiere Vd. otra cosa?	= Do you want anything else?
Nada más, gracias	= Nothing more, thank you.
No me gusta el clima de este país	= I don't like the climate of this country.
¿Qué haces, chico?	= What are you doing, child?

[1] Para (for, in order to) is used in such cases when a reason of some kind follows. If the English 'to' signifies 'in order to', then para should be used.

No hago nada en este mo- = I am not doing anything at this
mento, señor, pero más moment, sir, but, later on, I
tarde voy a jugar con mis am going to play with my
amigos friends.

¿Cuánto ha pagado su madre = How much has your mother paid
por aquellos huevos? for those eggs?

Dice que ha pagado demasiado = She says she has paid too much.

¿Cuál es el precio de esta = What is the price of this fountain
estilográfica pen?

No cuesta sino veinte pesetas = It costs only twenty pesetas.

La encuentro muy barata = I find it very cheap.

¿Qué le parece el tiempo? = What do you think of the
weather?

Hace muy mal tiempo = It's very bad weather.

¿Ha llegado el capitán? = Has the captain arrived?

Sí, ha llegado anoche = Yes, he (has) arrived last night.

¿A qué hora? = At what time?

A las diez y media = At half-past ten.

¿Ha llegado solo? = Did he arrive alone?

No solo, sino con dos otros = Not alone, but with two other
señores y una señorita gentlemen and a young lady.

¿Es su hija, la señorita? = Is the young lady his daughter?

Creo que sí = I believe so.

¿No está Vd. seguro? = Are you not sure?

No, señor, no estoy seguro = No, sir, I'm not sure.

¿Por qué no está Vd. seguro? = Why aren't you sure?

Porque no he hablado ni con el = Because I have not spoken either
señor ni con la señorita to the gentleman or to the
young lady.

Dígame, ¿cuándo partirá? = Tell me, when will he leave?

Creo que partirá mañana por = I believe he will leave tomorrow
la mañana morning.

¿Cuántos criados ha traído = How many servants has he
consigo? brought with him?

No los he visto = I haven't seen them.

¿Adónde va mañana? ¿Lo sabe = Where is he going to tomorrow?
Vd.? Do you know?

Sí, lo sé. Va al campo	= Yes, I know. He is going into the country.
¿En qué día de la semana estamos? ¿Puede Vd. decírmelo?	= What is the day of the week? Can you tell me?
Sí, señora, con mucho gusto. Hoy es miércoles	= Yes, madam, with pleasure. Today is Wednesday.
¿Cuáles son los nombres de los días de la semana? ¿Puede Vd. decírmelos?	= What are the names of the days of the week? Can you tell me them?
Son 'lunes, martes, miércoles, jueves, viernes, sábado y domingo'	= They are 'Monday, Tuesday, Wednesday, Thursday, Friday, Saturday, and Sunday'.
¿Y cuáles son los nombres de los meses del año?	= And what are the names of the months of the year?
Son 'enero, febrero, marzo, abril, mayo, junio, julio, agosto, septiembre, octubre, noviembre, y diciembre'	= They are 'January, February, March, April, May, June, July, August, September, October, November, and December'.

VII

THE FIFTH LESSON

The Imperfect Tense

hablar	temer	permitir
hablaba (I spoke, was speaking)	**temía** (I feared, was fearing)	**permitía** (I permitted, was permitting)
hablabas	**temías**	**permitías**
hablaba	**temía**	**permitía**
hablábamos	**temíamos**	**permitíamos**
hablabais	**temíais**	**permitíais**
hablaban	**temían**	**permitían**

The imperfect is the most regular of tenses, and verbs which are irregular in other tenses form their imperfect regularly, in accordance with their infinitive endings. The only three exceptions are:

ser	ir	ver
era	iba	veía
eras	ibas	veías
era	iba	veía
éramos	íbamos	veíamos
erais	ibais	veíais
eran	iban	veían

The Preterite Tense

hablar	temer	permitir
hablé (I spoke)	**temí** (I feared)	**permití** (I permitted)
hablaste	**temiste**	**permitiste**
habló	**temió**	**permitió**
hablamos	**temimos**	**permitimos**
hablasteis	**temisteis**	**permitisteis**
hablaron	**temieron**	**permitieron**

56

Whereas the imperfect is the tense in which fewest verbs are irregular, the preterite, or past definite (sometimes called the past historic), has the greatest number of irregularities. The uses of the two tenses will be discussed later, but the student should realize that the preterite corresponds to the simple past tense in English, and is in much more common use than the perfect. Great care should therefore be taken in learning this tense.

Irregular preterites are as follows:

haber	*tener*	*ser*	*estar*
hube	tuve	fui	estuve
hubiste	tuviste	fuiste	estuviste
hubo	tuvo	fue	estuvo
hubimos	tuvimos	fuimos	estuvimos
hubisteis	tuvisteis	fuisteis	estuvisteis
hubieron	tuvieron	fueron	estuvieron

ir (to go)	*venir* (to come)	*poder* (to be able)	*saber* (to know)
fui	vine	pude	supe
fuiste	viniste	pudiste	supiste
fue	vino	pudo	supo
fuimos	vinimos	pudimos	supimos
fuisteis	vinisteis	pudisteis	supisteis
fueron	vinieron	pudieron	supieron

querer (to wish, love)	*hacer* (to do, make)	*poner* (to put, place)	*decir* (to say, tell)
quise	hice	puse	dije
quisiste	hiciste	pusiste	dijiste
quiso	hizo	puso	dijo
quisimos	hicimos	pusimos	dijimos
quisisteis	hicisteis	pusisteis	dijisteis
quisieron	hicieron	pusieron	dijeron

dar (to give)	*ver* (to see)	*traer* (to bring)	*oir* (to hear)
di	vi	traje	oí
diste	viste	trajiste	oíste
dio	vio	trajo	oyó
dimos	vimos	trajimos	oímos
disteis	visteis	trajisteis	oísteis
dieron	vieron	trajeron	oyeron

andar (to go, walk)	*pedir* (to ask for)	*sentir* (to feel, perceive)
anduve	pedí	sentí
anduviste	pediste	sentiste
anduvo	pidió	sintió (i instead of e)
anduvimos	pedimos	sentimos
anduvisteis	pedisteis	sentisteis
anduvieron	pidieron	sintieron (i instead of e)

dormir (to sleep)	*caer* (to fall)
dormí	caí
dormiste	caíste
durmió	cayó
dormimos	caímos
dormisteis	caísteis
durmieron	cayeron

It will be noted that the preterite of **ser** is the same as that of **ir**. However, the context will always make clear which meaning is the correct one.

Caer is given here as an example of the type of verb ending in **-er** or **-ir** in which the stem ends in a vowel. Common verbs similar to it are **leer** (to read) and **huir** (to flee).

Note also that verbs ending in **-ducir** behave in the preterite like:

conducir (to lead, drive)
conduje
condujiste
condujo
condujimos
condujisteis
condujeron

Use of the Imperfect and Preterite Tenses

In general, the imperfect refers to an action which was proceeding or used to proceed, without a definite conclusion being suggested, whereas the preterite refers to an action which occurred once or a definite number of times and which was concluded. The following examples should be studied:

íbamos al cine cada semana	= we used to go to the cinema every week
almorzábamos a la una	= we had (used to have) lunch at one o'clock
leía un periódico cuando llegó su amigo	= he was reading a newspaper when his friend arrived
no estaba en casa cuando llamamos	= he was not at home when we rang
le vi ayer	= I saw him yesterday
estuve en Madrid el mes pasado	= I was in Madrid last month
fui a visitarle tres veces	= I went to visit him three times
almorzamos ayer a la una	= we had lunch yesterday at one o'clock

The Conditional

hablar	*temer*	*permitir*
hablaría	**temería**	**permitiría**
hablarías	**temerías**	**permitirías**
hablaría	**temería**	**permitiría**
hablaríamos	**temeríamos**	**permitiríamos**
hablaríais	**temeríais**	**permitiríais**
hablarían	**temerían**	**permitirían**

Like the future, the conditional is formed by adding endings to the infinitive. The endings are the same for all verbs, but those verbs which change their stems for the formation of the future do the same for the conditional (*tener*, **tendría**, *poner*, **pondría**, etc.).

The meaning of **yo hablaría** is 'I would speak' or 'I should speak'. When 'should' means 'ought to' the conditional of **deber** must be used, as follows:

yo debería ir a verle = I should (ought to) go and see him

Vds. deberían llegar para las ocho = you should (ought to) arrive by eight o'clock

Now let us learn by heart—**de memoria**—as the Spanish say, this little poem; it contains some useful constructions·

> Pobre flor que ayer naciste,
> ¡Cuán temprana fue tu suerte!
> Al primer paso que diste
> Te encontraste con la muerte.
>
> El llevarte es cosa triste;
> El dejarte es cosa fuerte;
> El dejarte con la vida
> Es dejarte con la muerte.

The translation runs:

> Poor flower that wast born yesterday,
> How soon came (was) thy fate!
> At the first step thou tookest (gavest)
> Thou metst with death.
>
> Taking thee away is a sad thing;
> Leaving thee is a strong (noble) thing;
> Leaving thee with life
> Is to leave thee with death.

There are three examples of the preterite in these lines, namely:

naciste, from **nacer** (to be born)
diste, from **dar** (to give)
te encontraste con, from **encontrarse con** (to meet with)

There are also two examples of infinitives used substantively:

(1) **el dejar** (the leaving)
   el dejarte (the leaving thee)
(2) **el llevar** (the taking away)
   el llevarte (the taking thee away)

Cuán is an adverb signifying 'how', as above.

Primero means 'first'; the feminine form is **primera**; the plural **primeros, primeras.** The final vowel is omitted before a masculine singular noun.

Reflexive Verbs

Reflexive verbs are, of course, conjugated in the same way as other verbs, the only difference being that the appropriate reflexive pronoun is placed before the verb (or after the verb if it is an infinitive, affirmative imperative, or 'gerundio').

levantarse (to get up, stand up)

yo me levanto
tú te levantas
Vd. se levanta
él, ella se levanta
nosotros nos levantamos
vosotros os levantáis
Vds. se levantan
ellos, ellas se levantan

Note the imperatives:

levántate (tú)	no te levantes
levántese (Vd.)	no se levante
levantémonos	no nos levantemos
levantaos	no os levantéis
levántense (Vds.)	no se levanten

It will be observed that in the **nosotros** and **vosotros** forms the last letter of the verb is dropped before the addition of the reflexive pronoun in the affirmative imperative.

The use of the reflexive verb may sometimes give rise to ambiguity. For instance, **se miran** could mean 'they look at themselves' or 'they look at each other'. Usually the context will make the meaning clear, but otherwise it is necessary to clarify the expression, as follows:

se miran el uno al otro	= they look at each other
se miran a sí mismos	= they look at themselves
se miran unos a otros	= they look at one another
nos miramos a nosotros mismos	= we look at ourselves

An important use of the reflexive is to render an English passive expression, the passive being comparatively rare in Spanish. There are two constructions, one for use when referring to things, the other when referring to persons.

1. **se habla español en Chile** = Spanish is spoken in Chile

   se cierran las puertas a las ocho = the doors are shut at eight o'clock

   se colocaron los sombreros en la mesa = the hats were placed on the table

2. **se me dice que no vendrán** = I am told that they will not be coming

   se le vio entrar en el museo = he was seen going into the museum

   se les despertó temprano = they were awoken early

In the first construction the subject is the same as the English subject, and the verb agrees with it; in the second, the English subject becomes the object and the verb is always in the third person singular, agreeing with the subject **se**.

The passive in Spanish is formed with **ser** and the past participle of the verb in question, and is chiefly used when we are told by whom or by what an action is performed.

la puerta fue cerrada por el portero = the door was closed by the porter

el pueblo fue destruido por el huracán = the town was destroyed by the hurricane

The Spanish language, as I have said in Lesson Three, is rich in suffixes.

FURTHER EXAMPLES

Un niño muy pequeño es pequeñito [1] = A very small child is a little one (mite, etc.).

Un libro pequeño es un librito = A little book is a booklet.

Una estatua baja es una estatuita = A low (small) statue is a statuette.

Una mujer muy baja es una mujercita = A very small woman is a little woman.

Un joven de poca edad es un jovencito = A youth of little age is a mere child.

Un árbol de poca altura es un arbolillo = A tree of little height is a sapling, etc.

Hijita de mi alma = Little daughter of my heart.[2]

Now I intend to tell a short story, first in English in order that you may realize its purport, and afterwards in Spanish. Endeavour by means of the English rendering to establish the idea of the story in your mind without special attention to the English words employed; but pay strict attention to every Spanish word.

English Version

Louis XIV asked one of his courtiers if he knew the Castilian tongue.

'No, sir,' replied the gentleman, 'but I'll learn it.' He worked with much careful attention (application) in order to learn the language quickly, because he thought that the king had the intention of appointing him ambassador in the court of Spain,

---

[1] Both nouns and adjectives may take these suffixes.
[2] Literally, 'soul'; **el corazón** is 'heart'.

and after a few months he went to tell the monarch that, now already, he knew the Castilian tongue.

'Very well,' replied the king to him, 'and I give you my congratulations, for you will be able to read *Don Quijote* in the original.'

Spanish Version

Luis XIV preguntó a uno de sus cortesanos si sabía el castellano.

—No, Señor,— respondió el caballero, —pero lo aprenderé.

Trabajó con mucho esmero para aprender pronto aquel idioma, porque pensaba que el rey tenía intención de nombrarle embajador en la corte de España, y después de unos meses fue a decir al monarca que ahora ya sabía el castellano.

—Muy bien,— le respondió el rey, —y le doy a Vd. la enhorabuena, pues podrá leer *el Quijote* en el original.

Here is another anecdote:

'I don't know how to get rid of Augustus; every day he comes to ask me for money.'

'And do you give him some?'

'No, but his presence inconveniences me.'

'Do you wish not to see him again?—Lend him five "duros".' [1]

The Spanish is rendered thus:

—No sé cómo librarme de Agustín; todos los días viene a pedirme dinero.

—¿Y tú se lo das?

—No, pero me incomoda su presencia.

—¿Quieres no volverlo a ver?—Préstale cinco duros.

The above passages, and, indeed, every other anecdote and story that may henceforth appear, should be recited aloud, not once, but many times; and such recitation must not be monotonous, but full of expression. Neither must they be recited until the idea of the whole is understood, nor without an increased

---

[1] A **duro** is worth five pesetas.

mobility of the organs of speech. Speak slowly and deliberately, and, above all things, with perfect confidence.

Now, here is a short poem which it would be wise on the student's part to commit to memory; indeed, all the extracts, stories, and poems, together with the 'Conversational Matter', should be read aloud, for this is the only course to adopt if the student wishes to become fluent in the language. I do not mean that one should learn them as a task, but rather as a pleasure, not by effort and strained concentration, but by familiarity, by reading them aloud with expression over and over again during a long period. In this manner impressions may be better preserved.

El dos de Mayo [1]

Este es el día en que, con voz tirana,
—Ya sois esclavos,— la Ambición [2] gritó.
Y el noble pueblo que lo oyó indignado
—Muertos, sí,— dijo, —pero esclavos, no.

The translation of the above runs:

This is the day in which, with tyrant voice,
'Already (now) you are slaves,' Ambition cried.
And the noble people that heard it, indignant—
'Dead, yes,' it said, 'but slaves, no!'

[1] 'The Second of May,' by Arriaza.
[2] A reference to Napoleon and the French domination in Madrid.

VIII

THE SIXTH LESSON

LET me now tell you another story, first in English in order that you may seize the idea of the whole, and then in Spanish so that the text may convey the same idea to your mind. When once you understand an idea that is to be expressed, endeavour to forget temporarily the words and phrases of the English version and concentrate upon the Spanish. This is the best way to learn.

A prince, wishing to amuse himself at the expense of one of his courtiers whom he had employed in different embassies, told him one day that with his big eyes and long neck he seemed, at the same time, like an owl and a goose.

'I do not know, sir,' replied the gentleman, with much dignity, 'whom or what I resemble, but I know very well that I had many times the honour to represent Your Majesty in several foreign courts.'

Here is the same story told in Spanish:

Un príncipe, queriendo divertirse a costa de uno de sus cortesanos a quien había empleado en diferentes embajadas, le dijo un día que con sus grandes ojos y largo cuello se parecía a la vez a un buho y a un ganso.

—Yo no sé, Señor,— le respondió el caballero con mucha dignidad, —a quién o a qué me parezco, pero sé muy bien que tuve muchas veces el honor de representar a Vuestra Majestad en varias cortes extranjeras.

Some verbs are used before the infinitive of other verbs without the intervention of a preposition. The most common are:

querer (to want)   **lograr** (to succeed in)
desear (to want)   **necesitar** (to need)
poder (to be able)   **olvidar** (to forget)
saber (to know how to, be able to)   **pensar** (to intend)

deber (to have to, must)	**permitir** (to permit)
conseguir (to succeed in)	**preferir** (to prefer)
decidir (to decide)	**prometer** (to promise)
dejar (to allow)	**soler** (to be accustomed to)
esperar (to hope)	**temer** (to be afraid of)
fingir (to pretend)	**recordar** (to remember)

ella sabe tocar el piano	= she can (knows how to) play the piano
logró ganar el premio	= he succeeded in winning the prize
pensamos ir a España este año	= we intend to go to Spain this year
prometió ir a buscarlo	= he promised to go and fetch it

Other verbs require a preposition, and a list of the more common ones, with the appropriate preposition, is given below.

apresurarse a (to hurry)	**convidar a** (to invite)
correr a (to run)	**forzar a** (to force)
enviar a (to send)	**incitar a** (to incite)
ir a (to go)	**instar a** (to urge)
salir a (to go out)	**invitar a** (to invite)
venir a (to come)	**obligar a** (to oblige)
volver a [1] (to return)	**persuadir a** (to persuade)
empezar a ⎫	**acertar a** (to succeed)
principiar a ⎬ (to begin)	**aprender a** (to learn)
comenzar a ⎭	**atreverse a** (to dare)
ayudar a (to help)	**enseñar a** (to teach)
ofrecerse a (to offer)	**resistirse a** (to resist)
acabar de [2] (to finish)	**acordarse de** (to remember)
alegrarse de (to be glad)	**cansarse de** (to weary)
cesar de (to stop)	**dejar de** (to omit; to cease)

[1] **volver a** is also used idiomatically to mean 'to do something again':

  volvió a leer la novela = he read the novel again

[2] **acabar de** also means 'to have just done something':

  acabamos de llegar = we have just arrived
  acababan de verlo = they had just seen it

guardarse de (to beware)	**olvidarse de** (to forget)
terminar de (to finish)	**tratar de** (to try)
consentir en (to consent)	**consistir en** (to consist)
convenir en (to agree)	**divertirse en** (to enjoy oneself)
empeñarse en (to insist)	**insistir en** (to insist)
persistir en (to persist)	**quedar en** (to agree)
tardar en (to delay, take time)	**vacilar en** (to hesitate)
amenazar con (to threaten)	**servir para** (to serve)
soñar con (to dream)	

corrió a ayudarle	= he ran to help him
le invité a visitarnos	= I invited him to visit us
aprende a hablar español	= he is learning to speak Spanish
se alegra de verlos	= he is glad to see them
no deje Vd. de venir a verme	= don't fail to come and see me
tardó diez minutos en llegar aquí	= it took him ten minutes to get here

There are also differences between Spanish and English verbs in the manner they are used with noun and pronoun objects. Verbs requiring a preposition in English but not in Spanish are:

aprovechar (to make use of)	**buscar** (to look for)
escuchar (to listen to)	**esperar** (to wait for)
mirar (to look at)	**pagar** (to pay for)

está buscando sus gafas	= he is looking for his glasses
esperamos la hora de comer	= we are waiting for lunchtime

Verbs which have no preposition in English but which require one in Spanish are:

acercarse a (to approach)	**acordarse de** (to remember)
carecer de (to lack)	**casarse con** (to marry)
disfrutar de (to enjoy)	**entrar en** (to enter)
gozar de (to enjoy)	**jugar a** (to play)
parecerse a (to resemble)	**reparar en** (to notice)

se casó con la hija del cartero = he married the postman's daughter
entraron en la iglesia   = they entered the church
juegan al fútbol   = they are playing football

The Subjunctive

The present subjunctive is formed thus:

hablar	*temer*	*permitir*
hable	**tema**	**permita**
hables	**temas**	**permitas**
hable	**tema**	**permita**
hablemos	**temamos**	**permitamos**
habléis	**temáis**	**permitáis**
hablen	**teman**	**permitan**

The general rule which covers nearly all verbs, regular and irregular, is that for the **o** of the first person singular of the present indicative are substituted **e**, etc., for **-ar** verbs, and **a**, etc., for **-er** and **-ir** verbs.

Exceptions to this rule are:

ser	**sea, seas, sea, seamos, seáis, sean**
estar	**esté, estés, esté, estemos, estéis, estén**
haber	**haya, hayas, haya, hayamos, hayáis, hayan**
ir	**vaya, vayas, vaya, vayamos, vayáis, vayan**
dar	**dé, des, dé, demos, deis, den**
saber	**sepa, sepas, sepa, sepamos, sepáis, sepan**

Also remember that spelling changes will be necessary in such verbs as **pagar** (**pague**), **buscar** (**busque**), **empezar** (**empiece**), **vencer** (**venza**), **coger** (**coja**), etc.

Finally, note the present subjunctive of radical-changing verbs which end in **-ir**.

pedir	**pida, pidas, pida, pidamos, pidáis, pidan**
sentir	**sienta, sientas, sienta, sintamos, sintáis, sientan**
dormir	**duerma, duermas, duerma, durmamos, durmáis, duerman**

The imperfect subjunctive is formed thus:

hablar	*temer*
hablase *or* **hablara**	**temiese** *or* **temiera**
hablases *or* **hablaras**	**temieses** *or* **temieras**
hablase *or* **hablara**	**temiese** *or* **temiera**
hablásemos *or* **habláramos**	**temiésemos** *or* **temiéramos**
hablaseis *or* **hablarais**	**temieseis** *or* **temierais**
hablasen *or* **hablaran**	**temiesen** *or* **temieran**

permitir

permitiese *or* **permitiera**
permitieses *or* **permitieras**
permitiese *or* **permitiera**
permitiésemos *or* **permitiéramos**
permitieseis *or* **permitierais**
permitiesen *or* **permitieran**

There exist two forms for historical reasons, and either form may be used. The rule for the formation of this tense has no exceptions: for the **-ron** of the third person plural of the preterite substitute **-se**, etc., or **-ra**, etc.

The perfect subjunctive is formed with the present subjunctive of **haber** and the past participle of the verb in question (e.g. *hablar*—**haya hablado, hayas hablado,** etc.) and the pluperfect subjunctive is formed with the imperfect subjunctive of **haber** and the past participle (e.g. *hablar*—**hubiese hablado, hubieses hablado,** etc.).

Uses of the Subjunctive

The student will remember that the present subjunctive is used as an imperative with **Vd., Vds.,** and **nosotros** (see the Third Lesson).

Otherwise it is a mood of the verb which is chiefly confined to subordinate clauses. It is generally used in statements which are doubtful or contrary to fact, and can usefully be studied under the following headings:

Noun Clauses. After verbs of wishing, doubting, and commanding, verbs of emotion and impersonal verbs:

queremos que Vds. vengan a visitarnos = we want you to come and visit us

dudo que lo haya terminado = I doubt whether he has finished it

le dije que viniese temprano = I told him to come early

siento que esté enfermo = I am sorry he is ill

es probable que llegue a tiempo = it is probable that he will arrive in time

importa que lo vean = it is important that they should see it

but note:

es verdad que vivía aquí = it is true that he used to live here

(Here the subordinate clause states what is a fact, and the indicative is used.)

Adjectival Clauses. After negative or indefinite antecedents:

no conozco a nadie que pueda ayudarme = I do not know anyone who can help me

quisiera encontrar un hombre que pueda hacer eso = I should like to find a man who can do that

Note also the following constructions:

cualquiera que sea su opinión } = whatever his opinion may be
sea la que sea su opinión

Adverbial Clauses. The subjunctive is always required after the following conjunctions:

antes (de) que	= before
para que	= in order that
sin que	= without
a menos que	= unless
como si	= as though
con tal que	= provided that

salí sin que me viese = I went out without his seeing me

lo haré con tal que Vd. venga conmigo = I shall do it provided you come with me

With other conjunctions, the mood of the verb will depend on whether the subordinate clause states a fact or not.

daban las cinco cuando llegó = it was striking five o'clock when he arrived

le veré cuando llegue = I shall see him when he arrives (but he has not arrived yet)

luego que vino almorzamos = as soon as he came we had lunch

luego que venga almorzaremos = as soon as he comes we shall have lunch (but he has not come yet)

lo hice, aunque sabía que era peligroso = I did it, although I knew it was dangerous

lo haré, aunque sea peligroso = I shall do it, even if it is dangerous

Conditional clauses do not obey the usual rules for the use of the subjunctive. Clearly, any statement introduced by 'if' must be doubtful, but the subjunctive is used after **si** only when the following statement is contrary to fact. It follows that the subjunctive will never be used in the present tense after **si**, but only in the imperfect or pluperfect.

si yo tuviese bastante dinero, compraría un coche = if I had enough money I would buy a car (but I haven't)

si Vd. me hubiese dicho eso, yo no habría llegado tarde = if you had told me that, I should not have arrived late (but you hadn't)

but

si tengo bastante dinero, compraré un coche = if I have enough money I shall buy a car

no sé si podré ir con Vd. = I don't know whether I shall be able to go with you

Finally, note the following useful expression:

¡Ojalá que hubiese sabido eso! = I wish I had known that!
¡Ojalá que haga buen tiempo! = I do hope it will be fine!

CONVERSATIONAL MATTER

¿Por qué ha hecho Vd. esto? = Why have you done this?

Si yo lo hubiera sabido no lo = If I had known it I should not
habría hecho   have done it.

¿Quién era el médico del rey? = Who was the king's physician?

El médico del rey era inglés y = The king's physician was English
muy sabio   and very clever.

¿Quién es su hermana? = Who is her (his) sister?

Su hermana es actriz en un = Her (his) sister is an actress in a
teatro de Madrid   Madrid theatre.

¿Qué hay de nuevo, amigo? = What is the news, friend?

Nada que yo sepa = Nothing that I know of.

Si el tiempo no fuese tan malo, = If the weather were not so bad,
yo partiría esta tarde   I should depart this afternoon.

Su primo de Vd. estaba muy = Your cousin was very tired,
cansado, ¿no?   wasn't he?

Vd. es soldado, ¿verdad? = You are a soldier, are you not?

Mi hermano está aquí, ¿no es = My brother is here, isn't he?
verdad?

Cuando Vd. llame a la criada, = When you call the servant don't
no olvide que su nombre de   forget that her Christian name
pila es Catalina   is Katherine.

Mis alumnos están estudiando = My pupils are studying the
la historia de Francia   history of France.

¿De veras? = Really?

Sí. Más tarde estudiarán la = Yes. Later they will study the
historia y la geografía de   history and geography of Eng-
Inglaterra   land.

Mi madre quisiera que comiese = My mother would like me to eat
mucho, pero yo no tengo   a lot, but I have no desire to
ganas de comer   eat.

Si Vd. no hubiera comido tanta carne, no habría estado enfermo	= If you had not eaten so much meat, you would not have been ill.
Yo quisiera vivir en el campo	= I should like to live in the country.
Ayer por la tarde toqué el piano en mi cuarto	= Yesterday evening I played the piano in my room.
No es a Vd. a quien dirijo la palabra, sino a su amiga	= It is not to you I direct my conversation (word) but to your friend.
Distingamos siempre entre lo bueno y lo malo	= Let us always distinguish between good and bad.
Vds. serían alabados si fuesen más diligentes	= You would be praised if you were more diligent.
Quisiera que sus amigos de Vd. nos acompañasen hasta la iglesia de que hemos estado hablando	= I should like your friends to accompany us to the church of which we have been speaking.
Dígame Vd. señor, ¿es éste el correo?	= Tell me, sir, is this the post-office?
Sí, señor. Por aquí se entra	= Yes, sir. One enters here.
¿A qué hora quiere Vd. que venga?	= At what time do you want me to come?
A las tres, señor	= At three o'clock, sir.
Estaré aquí a las tres	= I shall be here at three.
No tengo nada que hacer	= I have nothing to do.
¿Qué tiene Vd. que hacer?	= What have you to do?
Tengo mucho que hacer	= I have a lot to do.
Vd. no tiene nada que temer	= You have nothing to fear.

(Note the use here of **que**.)

¿Va Vd. algunas veces al campo?	= Do you sometimes go into the country?
Sí, de vez en cuando	= Yes, sometimes (from time to time).
¿Qué hace?	= What are you doing?
Acabo de escribir una carta	= I have just written a letter.
Acabo de visitar a mi amigo	= I have just visited my friend.

Yo no tengo ningún amigo = I have no friend.

¡Qué lástima! = What a pity!

No comprendo (entiendo) lo = I don't understand what you say.
que Vd. dice

 (**lo que** means 'what' in the sense of 'that which'.)

Me gustaría mucho saber lo = I should very much like to know
que piensa Vd.   what you think.

¿Quiere Vd. saberlo? = Do you wish to know (it)?

Sí, quiero saberlo = Yes, I wish to know (it).

IX

THE SEVENTH LESSON

ADVERBS may be formed from adjectives by the addition, to the feminine form in **a**, of the suffix **-mente**, as explained in the 'Introductory Remarks' at the beginning of the book.

Other adverbs of importance, some of which have already been given, are:

abajo	= below, downstairs	**acá**	= here
acaso	= maybe, perhaps	**además**	= besides, moreover
adelante	= forward	**ahí**	= there
ahora	= now	**allá**	= there
antes	= before	**allí**	= there
apenas	= scarcely, hardly	**aquí**	= here
arriba	= above, upstairs	**así**	= thus
atrás	= behind	**aun**	= even
bastante	= enough	**aún**	= still; yet
casi	= almost	**bien**	= well
cómo	= how	**cerca**	= about, near
debajo	= underneath	**delante**	= opposite, in front
demasiado	= too much, too	**dentro**	= inside
despacio	= slowly	**después**	= afterwards
detrás	= behind	**donde**	= where
encima	= above	**entonces**	= then
fuera	= outside	**jamás**	= ever, never
luego	= then; soon	**lejos**	= far, afar
ni	= neither, nor	**mal**	= badly
poco	= little	**nunca**	= never
pues	= so; then	**pronto**	= quickly, soon
siempre	= always	**quizá, quizás**	= perhaps
también	= also	**sólo**	= only
ya	= already; now	**todavía**	= yet, still

Any other grammatical points that remain to be explained will be dealt with as we come across them.

It is advisable that the student should know all the previous work thoroughly.

A STORY

Decía una madre a su hijo de cinco o seis años de edad, para inducirle a que acabase su tarea, que «Nunca se debe dejar para mañana lo que se puede hacer hoy día».

—En este caso, mamá,— le respondió el chiquillo muy a propósito, —hemos de acabar hoy mismo lo restante del pastelillo, y no guardarlo para mañana.

Maravillada la madre con tal agudeza, le dio permiso de acabarlo.

Translation

A mother said to her son of five or six years of age, in order to induce him to finish his task, that 'Never must one leave for tomorrow that which one can finish today'.

'In this case, mamma,' replied the youngster, very appropriately, 'we must finish today the remainder of the cake and not leave it for tomorrow.'

The mother, marvelling at such acuteness, gave him permission to finish it.

Notes

The construction is different to that of English sentences, therefore study it with the utmost care, not only in this extract but in all those that follow.

Nunca se debe dejar signifies 'one never ought to leave'. Literally, 'It never ought to leave itself'.

Lo que means 'that which' or 'what'.

Se puede hacer means 'can be done'. Literally, 'can do itself'. These common reflexive forms must be carefully studied.

Acabar means 'to finish'. When followed by **de** and an infinitive it signifies 'to have just' done something.

A propósito means 'to the point' in this case; it also signifies 'on purpose'—*vide* next story.

A STORY

Un criado, algo tonto, tenía la costumbre de llevar al correo todas las cartas que encontraba en el escritorio de su amo. Un día echó al buzón una de ellas, que no tenía todavía el nombre ni las señas del destinatario.

Al volver a casa, su amo se irritó y le preguntó furioso, —Pero, bruto, ¿no veías que en el sobre faltaba la dirección?

—Bien lo vi,— contestó el pobre hombre, —pero creí que Vd. lo hacía a propósito, con objeto de callar el nombre de la persona a quien manda la carta.

Translation

A servant, somewhat foolish, had the habit of taking to the post all the letters that he found on his master's desk.

One day he put into the box one of them that had not yet the name or the address of the addressee. On returning to the house, his master became annoyed, and asked him angrily, 'But, you ass, did you not see that the address was missing from the envelope?'

'I saw it well,' replied the poor man, 'but I believed that you had done it on purpose, with the object of concealing the name of the person to whom you are sending the letter.'

Notes

Algo usually means 'something', but when used with an adjective it signifies 'somewhat', as **algo tonto** in the above story; 'somewhat foolish', 'somewhat stupid'.

Amo means 'master' or 'patron'; the feminine is **ama**.

Echar means literally 'to throw'.

Las señas. The word **seña** means 'mark, sign'; in the plural, as above, it signifies 'address'.

Volver means 'to turn, to return'. Note the use of the infinitive in **al volver**, signifying 'on returning'. Thus other infinitives may be employed.

Irritar alone means 'to irritate', but **irritarse** will naturally signify 'to irritate oneself', or 'to become irritable', or 'to get annoyed'.

Faltar means 'to lack'. One can say also **Me falta un lápiz,** meaning 'I lack a pencil' or 'I want a pencil'. '**¿Qué le falta a Vd.?**' means 'What is lacking to you?' or 'What do you want?'
Dirección means 'destination' or 'address'.
Contestar means 'to reply, answer'.
A propósito means 'on purpose'. *Vide* previous story.
Callar means either 'to be silent' or 'to conceal'.
Mandar means 'to send' or 'to order'.

THE RAINBOW (El arco iris)

El arco iris es producido por los siete rayos del prisma—

(1) Rojo,
(2) Naranjado,
(3) Amarillo,
(4) Verde,
(5) Azul claro,
(6) Azul oscuro, y
(7) Morado,

refractados por los vapores y lluvia que nadan en la atmósfera, y reflejados sobre una nube oscura. Así es que sucede siempre en tiempo lluvioso, y cuando el cielo está aún nublado por un lado, y el sol despejado por el otro, debiendo hallarse el observador entre la nube y el sol. La luna suele producir también el iris, igualmente que las grandes caídas de agua y cascadas, los ventisqueros, y las olas del mar.

Translation

The rainbow is produced by the seven rays of the prism—

(1) Red,
(2) Orange,
(3) Yellow,
(4) Green,
(5) Light blue,
(6) Dark blue, and
(7) Violet,

refracted by vapours and rain that swim (hang) in the atmosphere, and reflected upon a dark cloud. Thus it is that it happens always in rainy weather and when the sky is still clouded on one side and the sun clear on the other, the observer having to stand between the cloud and the sun. The moon is accustomed also to produce the rainbow, equally with great waterfalls and cascades, snowstorms and the waves of the sea.

Notes

Arco iris means 'rainbow'.

Producir means 'to produce'.

El prisma means 'prism'. Notice that, although it ends in **a**, it is masculine. All nouns of Greek origin ending in **ma** are masculine.

Other common colours than those already given are:

> **negro** = black
> **blanco** = white
> **pardo** = grey
> **marrón** = brown

El vapor means 'vapour, steam'.

Lluvia means 'rain'.

Llover is the verb 'to rain'.

Nadar means 'to swim'.

Así es means 'thus it is' or 'it is thus'.

Suceder means 'to happen'.

Lado means 'side'; **por un lado** is 'on one side'.

Despejar is a verb signifying 'to remove, to clear away' things which impede, such as obstructions and impediments.

Despejarse (note the **se**) means 'to cheer up' and 'to become clear' when speaking of weather.

Despejado is an adjective signifying 'smart, quick, sagacious', and also 'clear'.

Debiendo is the 'gerundio' of **deber**, meaning 'to owe'; it also means 'to have to, to be obliged to', and is therefore in English variously translated as 'must, ought', etc.

Suele is the third person singular of **soler**, meaning 'to be accustomed' to do a thing, so that in a past tense one might translate it by 'used to'. Another equivalent would be 'to be in the habit of'. This verb is followed by an infinitive.

Igualmente que I have translated by 'equally with', but other expressions would have rendered the text equally clear, such as 'just like' or 'the same as'.

Caída is 'fall' (noun), being derived from the verb **caer**, to fall.

Ventisquero is a 'snowstorm'. Other useful names among Nature's works are:

los astros	= stars (*generally*)	la erupción	= eruption
el cielo	= sky	el hielo	= ice
el cometa	= comet	la nieve	= snow
la estrella	= star	el valle	= valley
la naturaleza	= Nature	la roca	= rock
el planeta	= planet	el polvo	= powder, dust
el sol	= sun	la piedra	= stone
la salida del sol	= sunrise	el ecuador	= equator
la puesta del sol	= sunset	el desierto	= desert
la tierra	= earth	la arena	= sand
la colina	= hill	el clima	= climate
la montaña	= mountain	el rocío	= dew
el lago	= lake	la neblina	= mist
la isla	= island	la niebla	= fog
el norte	= North	el granizo	= hail
el sur	= South	el trueno	= thunder
el este	= East	el terremoto	= earthquake
el oeste	= West	el relámpago	= lightning
el eclipse	= eclipse		

A STORY

Dos muchachos que jugaban al pie de un nogal, hallaron en el suelo una nuez que se había caído del árbol.

—Es mía,— dijo uno de ellos, —pues yo he sido el que la he visto primero.

—No,— respondió el otro, —es mía, porque yo he sido el que la he recogido del suelo.

No pudiendo ponerse de acuerdo respecto al legítimo dueño de la nuez, ya estaban dispuestos a disputársela a golpes, cuando un joven que pasaba, habiéndose enterado del motivo de la querella, cogió la nuez, la partió y poniéndose en medio de los muchachos, les dijo, —Yo voy a poneros de acuerdo; la mitad de la cáscara pertenece al que la vio primero y la otra mitad al que la recogió del suelo. Respecto a la nuez, yo me la guardo en pago de la decisión que he dado. Este es,— añadió riendo, —el resultado usual de todos los pleitos.

Translation

Two boys who were playing at the foot of a walnut-tree found on the ground a walnut that had fallen from the tree.

'It is mine,' said one of them, 'since it was I who saw it first.'

'No,' replied the other, 'it is mine, because it was I who picked it up from the ground.'

Not being able to come to an agreement as to the legitimate owner of the nut, already they were disposed to dispute it with blows, when a young man who was passing, having found out the reason for the quarrel, took the nut, cracked it, and, putting himself between the boys, said to them, 'I am going to bring you to an agreement; half of the shell belongs to him who saw it first and the other half to him who picked it up from the ground; regarding the nut (the inside), I am keeping it for myself in payment for the decision that I have given. This is,' he added, laughing, 'the usual result of all law-suits.'

Notes

Jugar means 'to play'.

Al pie de means 'at the foot of'.

Hallar means 'to find'.

El suelo means 'the ground'.

Caer means 'to fall'.

El que means 'he who' or 'that one which'.

Coger means 'to catch, seize'; and

Recoger means 'to pick up'.

Pudiendo is the 'gerundio' of **poder** (to be able).

De acuerdo signifies 'in agreement'.

Dispuesto is the past participle of **disponer**, meaning 'to dispose'; also 'to arrange, prepare'.

Disputársela means 'to dispute among themselves about it'.

Un golpe means 'a blow, a knock'.

Enterar means 'to acquaint, inform'; and

Enterarse will therefore signify 'to inform oneself', or, as we might say, 'to get to know'.

El medio means 'the middle'. **En medio de** will therefore signify 'in the middle of'. In this instance, I have translated it by 'between'.

Pertenecer means 'to belong'; also 'to appertain'.

Guardar means 'to keep', and also 'to put away'.

En pago de means 'in payment of'. The verb 'to pay' is **pagar**.

Añadir means 'to add'.

CONVERSATIONAL MATTER

¿A quién desea Vd. ver?	= Whom do you wish to see?
Deseo ver a mi tío	= I wish to see my uncle.
Pero no está aquí su tío	= But your uncle is not here.
¿Dónde está, pues?	= Where is he, then?
No sé, pero hace veinte minutos le vi cruzar la calle	= I don't know, but twenty minutes ago I saw him crossing the street.
¿Qué quiere Vd. hacer?	= What do you want to do?
Me gustaría mucho quedarme a comer con Vd.	= I should very much like to stay to dine (lunch) with you.

Note. Learn the following useful verbs, all beginning in **que-**:

quedar	=	to stay, stop
quemar	=	to burn
quebrar	=	to break
quejarse	=	to complain
querer	=	to wish, desire, want, love

¡Hasta la vista!	= Good-bye!
Mi amigo monta a caballo casi todos los días	= My friend goes riding nearly every day.

Note. **Montar a caballo** is equivalent to the French *monter à cheval*, and signifies 'to ride on horseback'.

¿No es la hora de volver a casa?	= Is it not time to return home?
Sí, lo creo	= Yes, I believe so.

Y también es la hora de acostarse	= And, also, it is time to go to bed.
Me voy a acostar	= I am going to bed.
Encienda Vd. la vela	= Light the candle.
Ayúdeme Vd. a desnudarme	= Help me to undress myself.
¿Dónde está el puente?	= Where is the bridge?
Queda [1] a cinco minutos de aquí	= It is (stays) five minutes from here.
¿Cuánto tiempo se tarda [2] a pie?	= How long does it take on foot?
Se lo he dicho a Vd.	= I have told you.
¿Conoce Vd. al señor Bustamante?	= Do you know Mr. Bustamante?
No, pero sé donde habita	= No, but I know where he lives.
¿Habita lejos de aquí?	= Does he live far from here?
O, sí, muy lejos	= Oh, yes, very far.
Volveré a verle a Vd.	= I shall come back and see you (*or* I shall see you again).
¿Qué día?	= What day?
Lunes, tal vez	= Monday, perhaps.

Now, before closing this chapter, let us learn the seasons, the days of the week, and the months of the year.

la primavera	= spring	el otoño	= autumn
el verano	= summer	el invierno	= winter
domingo	= Sunday	jueves	= Thursday
lunes	= Monday	viernes	= Friday
martes	= Tuesday	sábado	= Saturday
miércoles	= Wednesday		
enero	= January	julio	= July
febrero	= February	agosto	= August
marzo	= March	septiembre	= September
abril	= April	octubre	= October
mayo	= May	noviembre	= November
junio	= June	diciembre	= December

[1] Notice the use of the verb **quedar** here; it is frequently used thus.
[2] **Tardar** actually means 'to delay'.

X

THE EIGHTH LESSON

A STORY

YENDO un día de caza, el Rey de España, Carlos IV, se extravió por los bosques y, como tenía mucha hambre, entró en una pobre choza, donde se comió para cenar dos huevos escalfados.

—¿Cuánto te debo?— preguntó luego a la mujer que le servía.

—Dos mil reales, Señor,— contestó la astuta campesina.

—¡Demonio! ¡Qué raros serán los huevos en este país!

—No, Señor,— replicó ella, sonriéndose, —lo rarísimo es ver al Rey comer en nuestra cabaña.

Translation

Going out hunting one day, the King of Spain, Charles IV, lost his way in the woods, and, as he was very hungry, he entered a poor cottage, where he ate two poached eggs [1] for his supper.

'How much do I owe thee?' he presently asked the woman who served him.

'Two thousand reales,[2] sir,' answered the astute country-woman.

'The deuce! How rare eggs must be in this district!'

'No, sir,' she replied, smiling, 'what is extremely rare is to see the King eating in our hut.'

[1] huevos fritos	= fried eggs
huevos estrellados	= fried eggs
huevos revueltos	= scrambled eggs
huevos duros	= hard-boiled eggs
huevos pasados por agua	= soft-boiled eggs

[2] A former Spanish coin, worth a quarter of a peseta.

Notes

Yendo is the 'gerundio' of **ir**.

Caza means 'the hunt, chase'.

Extraviar means 'to mislead'; and

Extraviarse signifies 'to lose one's way'.

El bosque means 'the wood, forest, grove'.

La choza means 'a humble cottage'.

Cenar means 'to sup, to have for supper'; **la cena** is the evening meal corresponding to supper or dinner.

Luego means 'presently', and also 'then'.

Contestar means 'to answer, reply'.

El demonio means 'the demon'. It is here used as an exclamation.

Replicar means 'to reply'.

Sonreirse means 'to smile'. Notice that it is reflexive.

Rarísimo means 'extremely rare'.

Cabaña means 'a small cottage' or 'a hut'.

APPEARANCES

Cuando es de noche, parecen las estrellas en el cielo. De día hay también estrellas, pero la luz del sol no las deja resplandecer para nosotros. Cuando el sol se pone, va a alumbrar otros países. No se mueve él, sino la tierra. Cuando vamos en un coche muy de prisa, nos parece que los árboles caminan hacia atrás; del mismo modo, como nos movemos con la tierra, nos parece que el sol muda de lugar. Muchas cosas parecen verdades y no lo son. Por eso se dice que «las apariencias nos engañan.»

Translation

When it is night, the stars appear in the sky. By day there are also stars, but the sun's light does not let them shine for us. When the sun sets it goes to illuminate other lands. It does not move, but the earth (moves). When we go in a car, very fast, it seems to us that the trees are travelling backwards; in the same manner, as we are moving with the earth, it seems to us that the sun changes place. Many things appear truths and are not. Because of this it is said that 'appearances deceive us'.

Notes

De noche means 'by night' or 'in the night-time'.

Parecer means 'to appear, seem'.

De día means 'by day' or 'in the day-time'.

Dejar means 'to leave, let' and 'to allow'.

Resplandecer means 'to shine, gleam, glitter'.

Poner is the verb 'to put, place'.

Ponerse in reference to the sun signifies 'to set'.

Alumbrar means 'to light'; it also signifies 'to enlighten'.

Mueve is derived from **mover**, meaning 'to move'.

Sino, meaning 'but', is used after a negative when the meaning is 'but on the contrary'.

De prisa means 'quickly'; and

Muy de prisa signifies 'very quickly'.

Mismo means 'same'. When used with a pronoun it signifies 'self', as, for instance, **yo mismo** (I myself).

Mudar means 'to change, vary, alter'.

El lugar means 'the place, the situation'.

La verdad means 'the truth'.

Engañar means 'to deceive'.

AN ANECDOTE

Decía un andaluz, —Conocí a un hombre tan alto, tan grueso, y que pesaba tanto que cuando se murió tuvieron los sepultureros que hacer dos viajes para llevarlo al cementerio.

Translation

Said an Andalusian, 'I knew a man so tall, so corpulent (fat), and who weighed so much that when he died the bearers had to make two journeys to carry him to the cemetery.'

Notes

Grueso means 'fat' (of a human being).

Pesar means 'to weigh'; and

El pesar signifies 'sorrow, grief'.

Morir alone means 'to die'; and

Morirse signifies 'to die' and also 'to go out' in the sense of 'to be extinguished'.

Tuvieron is derived from **tener**, and **tener que** means 'to have to'.

El viaje means 'a journey'; and

Viajar is the verb 'to travel'.

Llevar means 'to carry' and also 'to wear', like the French *porter*.

AN AMUSING EPITAPH

Yace aquí Blas . . . y se alegra
Por no vivir con su suegra.

Translation

Here lies Blas . . . and rejoices
Through not living with his mother-in-law.

Notes

Yace is derived from **yacer**, meaning 'to lie'.

Alegrarse means 'to rejoice, to be glad'.

Por no vivir is, literally, 'through, by not to live'; freely it becomes 'because he isn't living with his mother-in-law'.

Suegra means 'mother-in-law; 'father-in-law' is **suegro**. Other human relationships and their intimate connections are: [1]

el soltero	= bachelor	el yerno	= son-in-law
el viudo	= widower	la nuera	= daughter-in-law
el huérfano	= orphan	el cuñado	= brother-in-law
el entierro	= funeral	la cuñada	= sister-in-law
la familia	= family	el matrimonio	= marriage
el abuelo [2]	= grandfather	el nombre de pila	= Christian name
el hijo	= son	los esponsales	= betrothal
el nieto	= grandson	la sociedad	= society
el sobrino	= nephew	el divorcio	= divorce
el primo	= cousin	el ciudadano	= citizen
el marido (esposo)	= husband	la vejez	= old age
		la juventud	= youth (period)
la mujer (esposa)	= wife	el nacimiento	= birth
los gemelos	= twins	la muerte	= death

[1] The feminine is generally formed by substituting **a** for **o** at the end of nouns.

[2] **El bisabuelo** means 'great-grandfather'.

The senses are:

la vista	= sight (*verb* ver)		el gusto	= taste (*verb* gustar)
el oído	= hearing (*verb* oir)		el tacto	= touch (*verb* tocar)
el olfato	= smell (*verb* oler)			

The principal psychological terms are:

el cariño	= affection		la alegría	= joy, gaiety
la ambición	= ambition		la gula	= gluttony, greediness
la amistad	= friendship			
el amor	= love		el odio	= hatred
la audacia	= audacity		el honor	= honour
la bondad	= goodness		la vergüenza	= shame
el carácter	= character		la ignorancia	= ignorance
la cólera	= anger		la imaginación	= imagination
la compasión	= compassion		la impudencia	= impudence
la conducta	= conduct, behaviour		la indignación	= indignation
			la inocencia	= innocence
la confianza	= confidence		la insolencia	= insolence
la conciencia	= conscience		la inteligencia	= intelligence
el temor	= fear		el interés	= interest
el crimen	= crime		la cobardía	= cowardice
la crueldad	= cruelty		la libertad	= liberty
la curiosidad	= curiosity		la memoria	= memory
el disgusto	= displeasure		el desprecio	= contempt
el despecho	= spite		la modestia	= modesty
la desesperación	= despair		la incuria	= carelessness
el deshonor	= dishonour		el orgullo	= pride
el deseo	= desire		la pereza	= laziness
la dignidad	= dignity		la pasión	= passion
la discreción	= discretion		la paciencia	= patience
el dolor [1]	= pain, ache		el pensamiento	= thought
la duda	= doubt		el miedo	= fear (*vide* temor)
el entusiasmo	= enthusiasm		la conmiseración [3]	= pity, commiseration
la envidia	= envy			
la esperanza	= hope		el placer	= pleasure
la altivez	= pride, haughtiness		la cortesía	= politeness
la adulación	= flattery, adulation		la previsión	= foresight
			la prudencia	= prudence
la fe [2]	= faith		el pudor	= shame, modesty
la franqueza	= frankness		la gratitud	= gratefulness

[1] El dolor de cabeza means 'headache'.

[2] ¡A fe mia! means 'Upon my honour!'

[3] Note that, in Spanish, one finds conm- where in English the 'mm' occurs.

el remordi-miento	= remorse	la sospecha	= suspicion
		la tristeza	= sadness
la simplicidad	= simplicity	la vanidad	= vanity
el cuidado	= care	la venganza	= vengeance
la necedad	= foolishness	la verdad	= truth

A JOKE

—¡Dime, hijo! Un hombre se cae al suelo desde un tejado y otro desde una silla. ¿Cuál es el que se hace más daño?

—El segundo, si la silla está en el tejado.

Translation

'Tell me, son! A man falls to the ground from a roof and another from a chair. Which is the one who hurts himself most?'

'The second, if the chair is on the roof.'

Notes

Desde, meaning 'since' (of time), also signifies 'from' (of place).

Daño means 'hurt, harm'.

Tejado means 'tiled-roof' or simply 'roof'.

A CHESTNUT

—¿Tienes buen sitio en tu clase?

—El mejor, papá—cerca de la estufa.

Translation

'Have you a good position in your form?'

'The best, papa—near the stove.'

A RIDDLE (IN VERSE)

Dicen que soy rey
Y no tengo reino.
Dicen que soy rubio
Y no tengo pelo.
Afirman que ando
Y no me meneo.
Arreglo relojes
Sin ser relojero.

Translation

They say I am a king
And I have no kingdom.
They say I am fair
And I have no hair.
They affirm that I walk (go)
And I do not move about.
I regulate watches
Without being a watchmaker.[1]

Notes

Rubio means 'fair', 'blond'. **Una rubia** is 'a blonde', and popularly
a **peseta**. **Tabaco rubio** is 'Virginian tobacco'.
Afirmar, meaning 'to affirm', also signifies 'to secure, strengthen'.
Menearse means 'to move', 'to stir'.
Arreglar means 'to arrange' or 'to regulate'.

A STORY

Cuando Boabdil, último rey moro de Granada, se vio obligado
a abandonar a España, terminada la guerra de la Reconquista, se
detuvo en la cumbre del monte Padul.

Desde aquel elevado sitio, descubríase Granada, la Vega y el
río Jenil, a orillas del cual se elevaban las tiendas de campaña
del ejército de los Reyes Católicos, Fernando e Isabel. A la vista
de tan bello país, que iba a abandonar para siempre, Boabdil
no pudo contener su emoción, y silenciosas lágrimas corrieron
por sus mejillas. La sultana Aïxa, su madre, que le acompañaba
en su destierro con los nobles que en otro tiempo componían
su brillante corte, le dijo, —Llora, llora, como una débil mujer,
la pérdida de un reino que no has sabido defender como hombre.

Pocos momentos después la hermosa Granada, último baluarte
de la dominación árabe en España, desaparecía de su vista para
siempre. Desde entonces aquel sitio se llamó y se llama aún hoy,
«El Suspiro del Moro.»

---

[1] The answer is **el sol** (the sun).

Translation

When Boabdil, the last Moorish king of Granada, was obliged to abandon Spain, the war of Reconquest being ended, he stopped on the summit of Mount Padul.

From this elevated spot there appeared Granada, the Vega, and the river Jenil, on the banks of which rose the tents of the army of the Catholic Rulers, Fernando and Isabel.

At the sight of such a lovely country, that he was going to abandon for ever, Boabdil could not contain his emotion, and silent tears ran down his cheeks. The 'Sultana' Aïxa, his mother, who was accompanying him in his exile with the nobles who in other days composed his brilliant court, said to him, 'Weep, weep, like a weak woman for the loss of a kingdom which you have not known how to defend like a man!'

A few minutes after the beautiful Granada, last bastion of the Arab domination in Spain, disappeared from his view for ever. Since then that place was called, and today is still called, 'The Sigh of the Moor'.

Notes

Terminada la guerra, etc. In this phrase, the participle must be understood as meaning 'being ended'. Notice particularly the construction in Spanish.

Detener means 'to stop, to detain'; and

Detenerse signifies 'to stop' or 'to tarry'.

Descubrir means 'to discover, uncover, reveal'; and

Descubrirse may be translated as 'to reveal oneself, to appear'.

La tienda may mean either 'the shop' or 'the tent'.

La orilla means 'the bank' of a river; and

El banco means 'the bank' of commerce.

Los reyes, literally meaning 'the kings', here signifies 'rulers' both the king and the queen.

Correr is the verb 'to run'.

La mejilla means 'the cheek'.

Componer means 'to compose'.

Llorar means 'to weep, to cry'. When used transitively, as in this context, it means 'to weep for, to bewail', or 'to mourn'.

Débil means 'weak'. Notice that the masculine and feminine forms are identical.

Aún means 'still, yet'. Without the accent it means 'even'.

The Principal Parts of the Body, etc.

la salud	= health	la oreja	= ear
transpirar	= to perspire, sweat	la ceja	= eyebrow
la transpiración	= perspiration, sweat	el párpado	= eyelid
		la pestaña	= eyelash
suspirar	= to sigh	la rodilla	= knee
el suspiro	= sigh	los nervios	= nerves
soñar	= to dream	el músculo	= muscle
el sueño	= sleep, dream	la carne	= flesh (*also* meat)
el hipo	= hiccough	la piel	= skin
gritar	= to cry out, shout	el corazón	= heart
bostezar	= to yawn	el hombro	= shoulder
el cadáver	= corpse	la cara	= face
la sangre	= blood	el rostro	= face
la cabeza	= head	el hígado	= liver
el cerebro	= brain	los pulmones	= lungs
la frente	= forehead	las espaldas	= back
el brazo	= arm	la costilla	= rib
la pierna	= leg	el vientre	= belly
la mano	= hand	el cuello	= neck
el pie	= foot	la boca	= mouth
el cuerpo	= body	el codo	= elbow
el pecho	= breast	el dedo	= finger
el estómago	= stomach	la uña	= nail (of finger or toe)
el hueso	= bone		
el esqueleto	= skeleton	el pulgar	= thumb
los cabellos (*plur.*)	= hair	la lengua	= tongue
		el labio	= lip
el ojo	= eye	el diente	= tooth
la mejilla	= cheek	respirar	= to breathe
la nariz	= nose	sollozar	= to sob

XI

THE NINTH LESSON

IN this chapter, for the sake of fostering interest, I intend to begin with a further selection of conversational matter which, as before, must be experimented upon by the student, new words being substituted for those given. Here is an instructive way of practising upon a sentence: Let us choose such an English one as 'I am going to town'. If we were teaching a foreigner we might give him the following variations:

Present: 'I am going to town today.'
Past: 'I was going to town yesterday.'
Future: 'I shall be going to town tomorrow.'
Conditional: 'I should be going to town, if . . .' [1]

According to the sense, we might continue thus—

Present: 'I often go to town.'
Past: 'I often went to town.'
Future: 'I shall often go to town.'
Conditional: 'I should often go to town, if . . .' [1]

Still further varying the meaning, we might continue indefinitely. Here, again:

Present: 'When I go to town . . .'
Past: 'When I went to town . . .'
Future: 'When I (shall) go to town . . .'
Conditional: 'If I should go to town . . .' [1]

This is how the student must work and form new phrases and sentences for himself if he wishes to attain fluency in any language whatever. To some students it may appear to be a very tiresome process, yet it ought not to breed discouragement, since it advances them upon their way. Both the analytic and synthetic

[1] Here, some reason or condition would follow.

methods must be practised if one wishes to make sure and steady progress. Therefore, it behoves one not only to read passages with the help of grammar and dictionary but also to form sentences with their help. The second is naturally the more difficult process, since both declensions and conjugations must be known with their respective irregularities. In language-study the predominant factor is undoubtedly patience; let the student of foreign idioms cultivate it. The reward is sure, and indeed worthy of attempt.

CONVERSATIONAL MATTER

¿Cuántos habitantes tiene España? = How many inhabitants has Spain?

No sé exactamente, pero creo que tiene unos veintinueve millones = I don't know exactly, but I believe about twenty-nine millions.

¿Tiene Vd. un despacho grande? = Have you a big office?

Mi despacho es un cuarto poco elegante pero uno de los más agradables del piso = My office is a room, not very elegant, but one of the most agreeable on the floor (storey of a building).

El habló sabia y elocuentemente = He spoke learnedly and eloquently.

Notes

Piso means 'storey, floor' and also 'flat'. Una casa de pisos is 'a block of flats'.

Sabia, if alone as an adverb, would have been sabiamente. When two adverbs, formed from adjectives, come together in the same sentence, as above, the first does not take the suffix -mente.

Mientras la mujer lloraba, el soldado reía = While the woman was weeping, the soldier was laughing.

En caso que yo esté ausente cuando venga su hermano de Vd., dígale que vuelvo al momento = In case I am out when your brother comes, tell him that I shall be back immediately.

¡Qué mal tiempo hace hoy! = What bad weather it is today!

Sí, pero hará peor mañana = Yes, but it will be worse to-morrow.

Ha venteado toda la noche = It has been blowing all night.

Sí, y está lloviendo ahora = Yes, and it's raining now.

Habiéndome paseado toda la mañana, tengo ganas de comer = Having walked all the morning, I have a great desire to eat.

¿Qué tiene Vd. ganas de comer? = What do you wish to eat?

No mucho; un poco de carne con pan = Not much; a little meat with bread.

Se dice que la virtud es mejor que el dinero, pero no todos lo piensan = It is said that virtue is better than money, but not everybody thinks so.

Después de haber oído al orador, quien habló clara-mente, pregunté su nombre, y me dijeron que era el Señor Rivera = After having heard the orator, who spoke clearly, I asked his name, and they told me that it was Mr. Rivera.

Habla bien este señor = He speaks well.

¿Un paseo tan corto le ha fati-gado ya? = So short a walk has already tired him?

Sí, me ha fatigado a mí también = Yes, and it has also tired me.

¿Está Vd. cansado? = Are you tired?

Sí, estoy muy cansado = Yes, I'm very tired.

¿A qué hora quiere Vd. comer? = At what time do you want to have lunch?

A la hora de costumbre, si le es igual = At the usual time, if it's all the same to you.

Pues yo prefiero comer media hora más tarde = Well, I prefer to eat half an hour later.

Notes

Me ha fatigado means 'it has tired me'. In English we would emphasize 'me' with an inflexion of the voice, but in Spanish it is necessary to add the emphatic **a mí**.

Es igual means literally 'it is equal', but is the usual expression for 'it's all the same'. **Me es igual** means 'it's all the same to me' or 'I don't mind'.

Este libro tiene el mismo tamaño que el otro =	This book is the same size as the other.
¿Sabe Vd. dónde vive el Señor Torres? =	Do you know where Mr. Torres lives?
Sé que vive en esta calle, pero no recuerdo el número =	I know that he lives in this street, but I don't remember the number.
¿Es casado? =	Is he married?
No estoy seguro, pero creo que no =	I'm not sure, but I believe not.

Notes

Recuerdo is derived from **recordar**, meaning 'to remind, remember'. There is another verb, used reflexively, **acordarse**, meaning both 'to come to an agreement' and 'to remember'.

Creo que no means 'I believe not' or 'I don't believe so'. Similarly, **creo que sí** would be 'I believe so' or 'yes, I believe so'.

AN EPIGRAM

—¿Qué hacías?— dijo Beltrán
A su mozo Juan Tabaco.
—Nada, señor.—¿Y tú, Paco?
—Yo estaba ayudando a Juan.

Translation

'What were you doing?' said Beltrán
To his servant Juan Tabaco.
'Nothing, sir.'—'And you, Paco?'
'I was helping John!'

THREE RIDDLES (*Tres adivinanzas*)

1. ¿En qué se parecen un guardia civil y un arco iris?
Ambos son signos de paz, y aparecen tras una tormenta, generalmente.

Translation

In what way do a civil guard and a rainbow resemble each other? [1]
Both are signs of peace, and appear after a storm (disturbance), generally.

2. ¿Qué es lo primero que hizo Napoleón cuando cumplió los treinta años?
Entrar en los treinta y uno.

Translation

What is the first thing that Napoleon did when he completed his thirty years (when he became thirty years old)?
Enter his thirty-first (year)!

3. ¿En qué mes hablan menos las mujeres?
En el de febrero.

Translation

In what month do women speak least?
In that of February!

PROVERBS (*Refranes*) [2]

Dime con quién andas, y te diré quién eres	= Tell me with whom thou goest and I will tell thee who thou art.
Nadie se muere hasta que Dios quiere	= Nobody dies until God wishes.
El hombre propone—y Dios dispone	= Man proposes—and God disposes.
El hábito no hace al monje	= Clothes do not make the monk.
El tiempo es oro	= Time is money.
Mala hierba nunca muere	= Weeds never die.

[1] Parecer means 'to appear, seem', and the reflexive form **parecerse** means 'to be like' or 'to resemble'. [2] 'Proverb' in Spanish is **el refrán**.

De noche todos los gatos son = At night all cats are grey.
pardos

Una golondrina no hace el = One swallow does not make a
verano   summer.

A buen entendedor pocas pala- = To an intelligent man a few
bras bastan   words suffice.

Más vale tarde que nunca = Better late than never.

Tanto va el cántaro a la fuente = The pitcher goes so much to the
que por fin se quiebra   fountain (well) that, in the end,
                                     it breaks.

Al hierro caliente—batir de = Strike while the iron is hot.
repente

De la mano a la boca se pierde = There's many a slip betwixt the
la sopa   cup and the lip.

La caridad empieza por uno = Charity begins at home (by one-
mismo   self).

Más vale un pájaro en la = A bird in the hand is worth two
mano que ciento volando   in the bush.

Notes

Muere is from **morir**, 'to die'.
Batir means 'to beat, strike'.
El cántaro means 'a pitcher, water-pot'.
La fuente means 'fountain'.
Por fin means 'in the end, at last'.
De repente means 'suddenly'.
Se pierde la sopa literally means 'the soup is lost'.
Ciento volando literally means 'a hundred flying'.

El refrán dice que nadie es = The proverb says that nobody is
profeta en su patria, lo cual   a prophet in his (own) coun-
sería verdad sin los ejemplos   try, which would be true with-
contrarios   out (if it were not for) the
                                     exceptions.

Casa tu hija como pudieres y = Marry your daughter as you can
tu hijo cuando quisieres   and your son when you wish.

Donde fueres, haz como vieres = When in Rome do as the Romans
                                     do.

Notes

In the last two proverbs are examples of the future subjunctive. This tense is rarely found outside proverbs and legal documents.

The literal translation of the last proverb is 'Wherever you go, do as you see'.

AN ANECDOTE

Hallaron tres hombres un tesoro; mas como no satisficiese el hambre que les acosaba, enviaron a uno de ellos a un pueblo vecino para que trajese algo de comer.

Cuando hubo comprado la comida el enviado, dijo para sí, —Si la enveneno, morirán sin duda mis dos compañeros, y el tesoro será mío por entero—. Y la envenenó.

Entretanto hablaban los otros dos hombres de esta manera: —Si le matamos cuando llegue, el tesoro será de los dos únicamente—. Y le mataron.

Comieron en seguida de lo que les había traído y murieron igualmente, tanto que el tesoro quedó sin dueño.

Translation

Three men found a treasure; but as it did not satisfy the hunger which troubled them, they sent one of themselves to a neighbouring village so that he might bring something to eat.

When the messenger had bought the food, he said to himself, 'If I poison it, my two companions, no doubt, will die, and the treasure will be mine entirely.' And he poisoned it!

Meanwhile the other two men were speaking in this manner: 'If we kill him when he arrives, the treasure will be for the two of us only.' And they killed him!

They ate afterwards of what he had brought them, and they died as well, so that the treasure remained without owner.

Notes

Satisfacer means 'to satisfy'; and
Satisfacerse means 'to satisfy oneself'.
Acosar means 'to molest', also 'to vex'.

Trajese is the imperfect subjunctive of **traer**.

Para que, meaning 'in order that', requires the subjunctive. **Para** alone (without **que**) is followed by the infinitive, as, **para traer**, meaning 'in order to bring'.

Algo means either 'something' or 'anything'.

El enviado from **enviar**, 'to send'. It is the past participle of the verb used as a noun. Therefore **el enviado** may be taken to mean 'the one sent'.

Envenenar means 'to poison'.

Sin duda means 'without doubt'.

Por entero means 'entirely' or 'wholly'.

Entretanto means 'meanwhile'.

De esta manera means 'in this manner' or 'in this way'.

Matar means 'to kill'; hence the word **matador** of the bullfight, meaning the 'killer'.

En seguida usually means 'immediately'. Here it may be taken to mean 'next' or 'afterwards'.

Igualmente means 'equally'. I have translated it as 'as well' in order to make sense.

Tanto que means 'so that' in this instance.

Plant Life

la violeta	= violet	el cedro	= cedar
el tulipán	= tulip	el castaño	= chestnut-tree [1]
el girasol	= sunflower	la higuera	= fig-tree [2]
la camelia	= camellia	el fresno	= ash
el lirio	= lily	el naranjo	= orange-tree [3]
la rosa	= rose	el ciruelo	= plum-tree [4]
el pensamiento	= pansy	el manzano	= apple-tree [5]
el crisántemo	= chrysanthemum	el peral	= pear-tree [6]
la lila	= lilac	el lúpulo	= hops
el abedul	= birch	el ananás	= pineapple
el haya	= beech	el albaricoque	= apricot
el sauce	= willow		
la encina } el roble }	= oak		

[1] 'A chestnut' is **una castaña**.   [2] 'A fig' is **un higo**.
[3] 'An orange' is **una naranja**.   [4] 'A plum' is **una ciruela**.
[5] 'An apple' is **una manzana**.   [6] 'A pear' is **una pera**.

Animal Life

el león	= lion	el lobo	= wolf
el tigre	= tiger	la zorra	= fox
el perro	= dog	el burro	= donkey
el caballo	= horse	la jirafa	= giraffe
el ciervo	= deer, stag	el elefante	= elephant
el conejo	= rabbit	el gato	= cat
la liebre	= hare	el ratón	= mouse

Bird Life

la gallina	= hen	la cigüeña	= stork
el gallo	= cock	el mirlo	= blackbird
el pollo	= chicken	el cuclillo	= cuckoo
el pavo	= turkey	el pavo real	= peacock
la tórtola	= dove	el cisne	= swan
la alondra	= lark	el cuervo	= crow
el buho	= owl	el gorrión	= sparrow
el ganso	= goose	la perdiz	= partridge
el águila (*fem.*)	= eagle	el buitre	= vulture
el ánade	= duck	el palomo	= pigeon
el faisán	= pheasant	el pájaro	= bird
la golondrina	= swallow	el ave (*fem.*)	= bird

Note that **pájaro** is generally used only of small singing birds. The generic term for birds is **ave**.

Fish Life

el pez	= fish	la sardina	= sardine
el salmón	= salmon	el pez de mar	= sea-fish
la anguila	= eel	el pez de agua dulce	= freshwater fish
la trucha	= trout		
la caballa	= mackerel	la ostra	= oyster
el lucio	= pike	la gamba	= prawn
la merluza	= hake		

Pez (*plural* **peces**) is the word for a live fish. Fish bought as food is **el pescado**.

XII

THE TENTH LESSON

EACH of the following sentences should be studied with the utmost care, since they contain much that is useful. They have been specially selected because they contain examples of grammatical constructions which have already been shown.

The subjunctive forms should be examined.

It is simple enough to memorize words, but the construction of a sentence is much more difficult. In the first case, the accidence must be well learned; in the second, one must endeavour to enter into the spirit of the language, to accept its mannerisms without comment at first. Learn a phrase and turn it about by substitution. Then repeat it aloud with emphasis, again and again. That is the secret of fluent speech.

CONVERSATIONAL MATTER

Mi hermano quiere que salga [1] con él = My brother wishes me to go out with him.

Tu padre suele [2] jugar al golf los sábados = Your father usually plays golf on Saturdays.

La hermana de mi amigo se sonríe cada vez que me ve = My friend's sister smiles each time she sees me.

Mi primo dice que ésta es la verdad y que el que diga lo contrario, miente = My cousin says that this is the truth and that anyone who says the contrary, lies.

Quisiéramos hacer un viaje a España, pero cuesta muy caro y como somos pobres, tendremos que renunciar a él = We should like to make a journey to Spain, but it costs a great deal and as we are poor we shall have to abandon it.

[1] **Salga** from **salir** (to go out). It is the subjunctive form after a verb of 'wishing', 'desiring'.

[2] **Suele** from **soler** (to be accustomed, to be in the habit of).

103

Quisiera que alguien me con- = I should like someone to conduct
dujese a la ciudad   me to the town.[1]

Me gustaría mucho visitarle a = I should very much like to visit
Vd.   you.

César vino, vio, y venció   = Caesar came, saw, and con-
quered.

Sería menester que Vds. diesen = It would be necessary for you to
la hospitalidad a su viejo   give hospitality to your old
amigo durante unos días a   friend for a few days at least.
lo menos

Hace algunos días di mi re- = A few days ago I gave my por-
trato a mi amiga pero no le   trait to my lady friend, but she
gustó   didn't like it.

No me gusta este libro   = I don't like this book.

Como relampagueaba mucho = As there was much lightning we
decidimos no salir   decided not to go out.

Después de habernos paseado = After having walked four hours
cuatro horas tomamos un   we took a taxi to return home.
taxi para volver a casa

No te atrevas jamás a ha- = Never dare to speak to me of
blarme de esto   this.

Esté Vd. persuadido de que = Be sure that you will be always
siempre será bien recibido   well received.

He tomado un baño y tengo = I have taken a bath and I'm still
calor todavía   warm.

Enrique Cuarto de Francia = Henry the Fourth of France was
fué asesinado en mil seis-   assassinated in sixteen hundred
cientos diez   and ten.

Hay hombres que saben ocul- = There are men who know how
tar en su interior todos los   to hide in their interior all the
apuros que les agobian y   griefs that oppress them and
por fuera siempre parecen   outwardly appear happy and
alegres y hasta chistosos   even humorous.

[1] 'I wish someone would conduct me to the town.'

Notes

Above all things the student must study very carefully—
analytically—the order of words in Spanish sentences so that he
may be able to express himself distinctly. As in all previous work,
so in the present, must he furnish himself with new sentences and
phrases by substitution.

Durante unos días means 'during a few days'. In English one says
'for a few days'.

Hace when used of 'time' means 'ago'.

Atreverse means 'to dare'; it is reflexive.

Todavía means both 'yet' and 'still'. This word is best studied
within a phrase or sentence.

Ocultar means 'to hide, conceal'. A common equivalent is **esconder**.

El apuro means 'grief, sorrow'.

Agobiar means in this case 'to oppress'; it also signifies 'to bend
down'.

Por fuera means 'outwardly'.

Chistoso means 'gay, lively', and 'humorous, funny'.

Un chiste is 'a joke' or 'witty saying'.

No me afeito nunca, porque no = I never shave, because I have no
   tengo barba   beard.

Notes

Afeitarse means 'to shave oneself'. For this operation one em-
ploys **una máquina de afeitar** (a razor), and **una brocha** (shaving-
brush), and, of course, **el jabón** (soap). The rest that is required
is **agua caliente** (hot water) and **una toalla** (a towel). An electric
shaver is **una máquina de afeitar eléctrica**. An open razor is **una
navaja**.

El tiempo y la temperatura = The weather and the tempera-
   varían mucho, según las   ture vary very much, according
   estaciones. Por no hacer   to the seasons. By not being
   fríos tremendos ni calores   tremendously cold or exces-
   excesivos, resulta la prima-   sively hot, spring is the most
   vera la más hermosa y más   beautiful and agreeable of all.
   agradable de todas

Notes

Según means 'according to'.

Por no hacer means 'by not being'; it may also signify 'by not making'.

Fríos and **calores** are in the plural; they signify 'colds' and 'heats'.

Resultar is often used with the meaning 'to be' or 'to turn out to be'.

A fines de septiembre se va el verano para dejar entrar el otoño =	About the end of September the summer goes away to let the autumn enter.

Notes

A fines de used in the plural, meaning 'about the end of'.

Se va from **irse** means 'to go away' or 'to go off'.

Para dejar entrar means 'so as to allow to enter'. The word **para** may be translated variously 'for', 'so as', or 'in order to'.

El invierno es la estación más fría y más triste del año =	Winter is the coldest and saddest season of the year.
En el colegio los alumnos hacen una figura de nieve, poniéndole una pipa en la boca =	In school the pupils make a snowman, putting a pipe into its mouth.
Entra el verano el 21 de junio y dura hasta el 25 de septiembre =	Summer enters on the 21st of June and lasts until the 25th of September.
Al llegar el verano, hace un calor sofocante =	On the arrival of summer the heat becomes suffocating.
¿Cuántos años hace que Vd. vive en Londres? =	How many years have you lived in London?
No más que dos años =	Not more than two years.
¿Dónde nació Vd.? =	Where were you born?
Nací en Madrid =	I was born in Madrid.

Hace tres años que vivimos en Londres = We have been living in London for three years.

Estudiamos el español desde hace seis meses = We have been studying Spanish for six months.

El barbero me ha cortado la mejilla con su navaja = The barber has cut my cheek with his razor.

Me duele la cabeza = My head aches.

Me duelen las muelas = My teeth ache.

Notes

Doler means 'to ache'.

The front teeth are **los dientes**. The back teeth are **las muelas**. 'Toothache' is **el dolor de muelas**.

El hijo fue enviado por su padre = The son was sent by his father.

El reloj perdido por mi madre fue hallado por mi prima = The watch lost by my mother was found by my cousin.

No creo que mi padre coja muchas uvas en su jardín este año = I don't think my father will pick many grapes in his garden this year.

Es preciso que los ladrones sean entregados a la justicia = It is necessary that the thieves be delivered up to justice.

Notes

Es preciso followed by the subjunctive, as above, means 'it is necessary'. As an adjective **preciso** means 'necessary, precise, exact'.

Entregar means 'to deliver, hand over'.

Entregarse means 'to deliver oneself up'.

¿Quién está ahí? = Who is there?

Soy yo,—no tenga Vd. miedo = It is I,—don't be afraid.

¿Dónde vive Vd.? = Where do you live?

En la esquina de la calle Alcalá = At the corner of Alcalá Street.

¡Viva la libertad! = Long live liberty!

¡Viva España!	= Long live Spain!
El año se divide en doce meses	= The year is divided into twelve months.
Los meses se dividen en cuatro semanas	= The months are divided into four weeks.
¿Y las semanas?	= And the weeks?
Estas se dividen en siete días	= These are divided into seven days.
Añadiendo dos a cuatro se obtiene seis	= Adding two to four, one obtains six.
¿Qué teme Vd.?	= What do you fear?
¿Yo?—No temo nada	= I?—I fear nothing.
Nuestros enemigos acometieron la ciudad hacia la media noche	= Our enemies attacked the town about midnight.
Todavía el marinero no me ha dado el mapa	= The sailor has not yet given me the map.
Si yo no hubiera gastado todo mi dinero, compraría un regalo para mi amiga	= If I hadn't spent all my money, I should buy a present for my lady friend.

Notes

Gastar means 'to spend' where money is concerned. 'To spend a fortnight' is pasar quince días.

Comprar means 'to buy'.

Un regalo means 'a present'.

Es preciso que Vd. esté en Londres de aquí a un mes	= You must be in London a month from now.
Mañana no estaré en casa a las nueve, sino a las diez y media	= Tomorrow I shall not be at home at nine, but at half-past ten.
¿Ha vendido Vd. algo?	= Have you sold anything?
No he vendido nada, pero he comprado doce huevos	= I've sold nothing, but I've bought twelve eggs.
La rosa es tan bella como la azucena	= The rose is as beautiful as the lily.

Aquel hombre ha sido el menos fiel de mis amigos	= That man has been the least faithful of my friends.
Londres es la más populosa de todas las ciudades de Europa	= London is the most populous of all the cities of Europe.
Mi hermana está enferma	= My sister is ill.
Lo siento mucho	= I'm very sorry.
Haga Vd. el favor de darme agua	= Please give me some water.
Esta casa es la [1] de mi hermano	= This house is my brother's.
No es de Vd. de quien hablo	= It is not you I'm talking about.
Será premiado por el profesor	= He will be rewarded by the teacher.
Le premiaré a él	= I will reward him.
Le he visto a Vd. muchas veces	= I have seen you many times.
No lo ha visto nadie ⎫ **Nadie lo ha visto** ⎭	= Nobody has seen it.
Es más viejo de lo que se cree	= He is older than one thinks.
Lo habrá visto	= He will have seen it. (He must have seen it.)
Lo habrá dicho	= He will have said it. (He must have said it.)
Quien calla, otorga	= He who is silent, consents.

Notes

'More than' before a noun or pronoun is **más que**. Before a numeral it is **más de**. In the example above the comparison is with a clause, and in this case it must be **más de lo que**.

¿Adónde piensa Vd. ir?	= Where do you intend to go?
Sólo a poca distancia de aquí	= Only a short way from here.
Lo espero	= I hope so.
También lo espero yo	= I hope so, too.

[1] Note the use of the article to express 'that' or 'the one'—'This house is that of my brother.'

A RIDDLE

¿Quién es el que, sin ceremonia y con sombrero puesto, se
sienta delante del rey, del Papa, del emperador o del presidente
de una república?—¡El cochero!

Translation

Who is it that, without ceremony and with hat on, seats himself
before (in the presence of) the king, the Pope, the emperor or the
president of a republic?—The coachman!

Notes

El que means 'he who', just as **lo que** means 'that which'.

El Papa is 'the Pope'; **el papá** is 'papa, father'; **la papa** means
'potato'.

Domestic Articles

el plato	= plate	la cubeta	= tub, barrel
la caldera	= kettle	el cesto ⎫	= basket
el tenedor	= fork	la cesta ⎭	
el cuchillo	= knife	la campanilla	= bell
la cuchara	= spoon	la alfombra	= carpet
la botella	= bottle	la silla	= chair
la servilleta	= serviette, napkin	la llave	= key
la taza	= cup	la lámpara	= lamp
el vaso	= glass [1]	el espejo	= mirror, looking-glass
la cerilla	= match		
la escoba	= broom	el canapé, el sofá	= couch, sofa
la cuna	= cradle	la jaula	= cage
la cama ⎫	= bed	la cortina	= curtain
el lecho ⎭		la caja	= box
el cojín	= cushion	el armario	= cupboard
la almohada	= pillow	la tetera	= tea-pot
el platillo	= saucer	el cuadro	= picture

[1] The material glass is **vidrio**.

Foods

el azúcar	= sugar	la galleta	= biscuit
el pan	= bread	el queso	= cheese
la mantequilla	= butter	el vinagre	= vinegar
el chorizo	= sausage	la cerveza	= beer
el carnero	= mutton	el vino	= wine
la carne de puerco	= pork	el caldo	= broth
		la ensalada	= salad
la ternera	= veal	el huevo	= egg
la vaca (carne de vaca)	= beef	la tortilla	= omelette, pancake
		el espárrago	= asparagus
la sopa	= soup	la conserva, la confitura	= jam
la mostaza	= mustard		
la sal	= salt	el tomate	= tomato
la pimienta	= pepper	el arroz	= rice
la patata	= potato	la leche	= milk
el cohombro	= cucumber	la nata, la crema	= cream
la torta	= cake, tart		

XIII

THE ELEVENTH LESSON

THOUGHTS

El estudio más útil es el de sí mismo.—*J. J. Rousseau.*
(The most useful study is that of oneself.)
Sólo es grande el que siente y practica la verdadera caridad.—
Kempis.
(Only he is great who feels and practises true charity.)
El porvenir del niño es obra de su madre.—*Napoleon.*
(The future of the child is the mother's work.)
El egoísta incendiara vuestra casa para cocer un huevo.—
Chamfort.
(The egoist would burn your house to boil an egg.)
**Nuestros mayores enemigos están con nosotros: son la ambición,
los celos y la avaricia.**—*Fenelón.*
(Our greatest enemies are with us: they are ambition, jealousy
and greed.)
Estudia para saber mejor y no para saber más que los otros.—
Seneca.
(Study in order to know better and not to know more than
others.)

GIBRALTAR

Siempre ha sido Gibraltar una ciudad comprimida. Pero con
ser mucha la aglomeración de hoy no es nada para el hacinamiento
de los años de la guerra. Hubo días en que el número de soldados
superaba a la población civil. Y ésta era por entonces de unas
17.000 almas. A ellas se añadían los diez o doce mil españoles
que hacen su jornada de trabajo en la plaza y salen de noche.
Ascienda o diminuya la guarnición o el vecindario, Gibraltar es

una ciudad sin ensanche y con un perímetro fijo. Cinco kilómetros escasos de largo por poco más de un kilómetro de ancho.

Se maravilla uno cuando sabe todo lo que puede caber en tan angosto y reducido espacio: un barrio comercial, 400 edificios gubernamentales, una Catedral, capillas católicas, presbiterianas, metodistas; sinagogas, hoteles, escuelas, internados, conventos, cementerios, jardines, Bancos, Tribunal de Justicia, teatros, cines, campo de fútbol, hospitales, bibliotecas, prisiones, centros benéficos, embalses, aeródromos, un castillo árabe, murallas, casamatas, torres ...

Pero todo esto en cierto modo es lo accidental o superfluo de Gibraltar. Lo fundamental y lo sólido, la razón de la existencia de Gibraltar son las obras militares que empiezan en sus contornos y se multiplican hasta los 425 metros de altura, sin repliegue, saliente o perfil al que no se le haya adjudicado misión. De esta manera se hizo de la roca la llave del Mediterráneo, se la convirtió en escudo, y en sus oquedades se ocultan baterías de cañones, puestos de antiaéreos, centrales eléctricas, estaciones de radar, nidos de proyectores, cisternas de carburantes, inmensos depósitos de municiones y víveres, carboneras para abastecer a un ejército y a las escuadras.

Una miniatura del poder de Inglaterra incrustada en una roca. Pero esto, en última instancia, sólo sería una arrogancia guerrera si el vigía de Punta de Europa no tuviera ante sus ojos—que son los ojos del Imperio—el espectáculo extraordinario y permanente que allí se ofrece. Punto de intersección de dos océanos y de las miradas de dos continentes se descubren al frente de las sombras violáceas de las costas de Africa. La emoción de que este cruce es uno de los pulsos del orbe, no basta: se complementa con el desfile incesante de barcos que resbalan por el horizonte. Mensajeros entre Oriente y Occidente, van o vuelven de la Europa mediterránea a las playas atlánticas. Cada uno es la página del libro donde están consignadas todas las flotas del mundo; estrofa de una poesía sin fin que compone la inquietud comercial y viajera del siglo.

Translation

Gibraltar has always been a compact city. But although the congestion nowadays is considerable, it is nothing to the over-crowding of the war years. There were times when the number of troops exceeded the civilian population. And the latter was then about 17,000 souls. To them were added the ten or twelve thousand Spaniards who do their day's work in the stronghold and leave at night. Whether the garrison or the number of residents increases or diminishes, Gibraltar is a city without possibility of expansion and with a fixed perimeter. A bare five kilometres long by a little more than one kilometre wide.

One is amazed when one knows all that can be contained in such a narrow and limited space: a commercial district, 400 government buildings, a cathedral, Catholic, Presbyterian, and Methodist churches; synagogues, hotels, day and boarding schools, convents, cemeteries, gardens, banks, Law Court, theatres, cinemas, a football ground, hospitals, libraries, prisons, welfare centres, reservoirs, aerodromes, an Arab castle, ramparts, casemates, towers . . .

But all this is in a way the accidental or superfluous aspect of Gibraltar. The fundamental and solid part, the reason for Gibraltar's existence, are the military installations which begin in its outskirts and pile up to a height of 425 metres, without a single hollow, salient, or contour which has not been allotted its purpose. In this way the rock was made the key to the Mediterranean, it was turned into a shield, and in its cavities are concealed batteries of guns, anti-aircraft positions, electric power stations, radar installations, searchlight batteries, fuel storage tanks, huge stores of munitions and provisions, coal dumps to supply an army and the fleets.

A miniature of England's power incrusted in a rock. But this, in the last resort, would be no more than aggressive arrogance if the watch-tower of Punta de Europa did not have in her eyes—which are the eyes of the Empire—the extraordinary and per-manent spectacle which is presented there. A point of intersection of two oceans and the outlook of two continents are discovered opposite the violet shadows of the African coasts. The feeling that this crossroad is one of the pulses of the world is not enough: it is complemented by the incessant passage of ships sailing over the horizon. Messengers between East and West, they come and go between Mediterranean Europe and the shores of the Atlantic. Each one is a page in the book where all the fleets in the world are inscribed; a verse of the endless poem composed by the restless commerce and tourism of the century.

A STORY

Se refiere una anécdota de un escocés que era oficial del ejército británico y fue mandado con su regimiento a Gibraltar.

En aquel entonces era subalterno y hallábase un día de guardia con otro compañero, el cual tuvo la desgracia de caer en un precipicio de cuatrocientos pies de profundidad, y quedó muerto.

Era deber del subalterno dar cuenta de lo ocurrido en la guardia, y habiéndolo hecho así, añadió la fórmula de costumbre, «Nada de particular ha ocurrido en la guardia.»

El fatal accidente de la caída llegó a oídos del comandante, y naturalmente la frase, de «nada de particular ha ocurrido» le causó extrañeza.

—¡Cómo!— exclamó, —¿llama Vd. eso «nada de particular,» cuando su compañero ha muerto, cayendo de una altura de cuatrocientos pies?

—Sí, señor,— replicó el subalterno, —no he creído que hubiera en ello nada de extraordinario. Si el pobre amigo hubiese caído en un precipicio de cuatrocientos pies, sin quedar muerto, sí que lo hubiera hallado muy extraordinario.

Translation

An anecdote is related of a Scotsman who was an officer of the British Army and was sent with his regiment to Gibraltar.

At that time he was a subaltern, and found himself one day on guard with a companion, who had the misfortune to fall over a precipice of a depth of four hundred feet, and was killed.

It was the duty of the subaltern to report the occurrence to the guard, and having done so, he added the customary formula, 'Nothing particular has occurred in the guard.'

The fatal accident of the fall came to the hearing of the commandant, and naturally, the phrase, 'Nothing particular has occurred', caused him astonishment.

'What!' he exclaimed, 'do you call this "nothing particular", when your comrade has died, falling from a height of four hundred feet?'

'Yes, sir,' replied the subaltern, 'I did not think there was anything extraordinary in it. If the poor friend had fallen over a precipice of four hundred feet, without being killed, indeed I should have found it very extraordinary.'

Notes

Referir means 'to refer, relate, report'. Therefore **se refiere** means 'it reports itself' or 'it is reported'.

Hallábase de guardia means 'he found himself on duty, on guard', or 'he was on guard, on duty'.

La desgracia means 'misfortune'.

Caer means 'to fall'.

Dar cuenta means 'to give account'. **Darse cuenta** means 'to realize'.

A oídos de means 'to the hearing of', or, as we should say, 'to the ears of'.

Sí que is an emphatic expression. In English we should merely stress the word 'should'.

COUNTRIES AND TOWNS

Europa	= Europe	**Holanda**	= Holland
Asia	= Asia	**Portugal**	= Portugal
África	= Africa	**Rusia**	= Russia
América	= America	**Suecia**	= Sweden
Australia	= Australia	**Turquía**	= Turkey
Inglaterra	= England	**Italia**	= Italy
Francia	= France	**Dinamarca**	= Denmark
España	= Spain	**China**	= China
Escocia	= Scotland	**Grecia**	= Greece

Los Estados Unidos	= The United States	Berlín	= Berlin
Irlanda	= Ireland	Viena	= Vienna
Noruega	= Norway	Varsovia	= Warsaw
Polonia	= Poland	Niza	= Nice
Suiza	= Switzerland	Nápoles	= Naples
Londres	= London	Moscú	= Moscow
París	= Paris	Milán	= Milan
Roma	= Rome	Lisboa	= Lisbon
Venecia	= Venice	Génova	= Genoa
Ginebra	= Geneva	Amberes	= Antwerp

MILITARY TERMS

el ejército	= army	el fusil	= rifle
el estado mayor	= staff	la ametralladora	= machine gun
la brigada	= brigade	la bomba	= bomb
la división	= division	la fortaleza	= fortress
el batallón	= battalion	la trinchera	= trench
el escuadrón	= squadron	la victoria	= victory
el regimiento	= regiment	la retirada	= retreat
el general	= general	la derrota	= rout
el coronel	= colonel	la batalla	= battle
el comandante	= major	la guerra	= war
el capitán	= captain	la mina	= mine
el teniente	= lieutenant	el parapeto	= parapet
el oficial	= officer	la pólvora	= gunpowder
el sargento	= sergeant	la pistola	= pistol
el soldado	= soldier	la bayoneta	= bayonet
la infantería	= infantry	el avión	= aeroplane
la caballería	= cavalry	el avión de reacción	= jet plane
la artillería	= artillery		
el centinela	= sentry	el cohete	= rocket
la espada	= sword	el caza	= fighter (plane)

MARINE TERMS

el ancla	= anchor	el piloto	= pilot
el navío	= ship	el capitán	= captain
la escuadra	= fleet	la vela	= sail
el remo	= oar	la brújula	= compass
el faro	= lighthouse	el babor	= port-side
el marinero	= sailor	el estribor	= starboard-side
la boya	= buoy	la balsa	= raft

el remolcador	= tug	el vapor	= steamboat
el buque de guerra	= warship	el camarote	= cabin, berth
la chimenea [1]	= funnel	los palos, los mástiles	= masts
el timón	= helm	la cubierta	= deck
la hélice	= screw (propeller)	la proa	= prow, head
el buque mercante	= merchant ship	la popa	= poop, stern
la amarra	= cable, hawser	la bomba [2]	= pump

TRADES, PROFESSIONS, AND DIGNITIES

el dentista [3]	= dentist	el banquero [5]	= banker
el barbero [3]	= barber	el rey	= king
el sastre	= tailor	la reina	= queen
el óptico	= optician	el príncipe	= prince
el pintor	= painter	la princesa	= princess
el joyero	= jeweller	el duque	= duke
el relojero	= watchmaker	la duquesa	= duchess
el panadero	= baker	el barón	= baron
el carnicero	= butcher	el conde	= count
el botero	= boot-maker	el marqués	= marquis
la lavandera	= washerwoman	el caballero	= knight, or gentleman
el abogado	= lawyer	el hidalgo	= nobleman
el juez	= judge	el embajador	= ambassador
el herrero	= blacksmith	la embajada	= embassy
el químico	= chemist [4]	la legación	= legation
el farmacéutico	= chemist, apothecary	el cónsul	= consul
el librero	= bookseller	el consulado	= consulate
el impresor	= printer	el gobierno	= government
el vendedor de comestibles	= grocer	el canciller	= chancellor
el profesor	= teacher, schoolmaster	el ministerio	= ministry
el lechero	= milkman	el ministro de guerra	= minister for war
el médico	= doctor (of medicine)	el ministro de Estado	= minister of state
el músico	= musician	el ministro de marina	= minister of marine
el albañil	= mason	el par	= peer

[1] Also 'the chimney'. [2] Also 'bomb'. [3] Or el peluquero (hairdresser).
[4] El químico signifies 'one who studies and perhaps teaches chemistry', and el farmacéutico is 'he who sells drugs and medicines'.
[5] 'The bank' is el banco.

el soberano	= sovereign	el abad	= abbot
el monarca	= monarch	el cura	= priest
la Cámara de los Comunes	= House of Commons	el obispo	= bishop
		el misionero	= missionary
la Cámara de los Pares	= House of Lords	el fraile (monje)	= friar (monk)
		el Papa	= the Pope
el alcalde	= mayor	el organista	= organist
el presidente	= president, chairman		

COMMERCIAL TERMS

el dependiente	= clerk, assistant	el giro postal	= postal order
el socio	= partner	la obligación	= bond
el recibo	= receipt	el pago	= payment
la factura	= invoice	el libro mayor	= ledger
el descuento	= discount	el detalle	= detail
la cuenta	= account	la exportación	= exportation
la venta	= sale	la deuda	= debt
la firma	= signature; firm	el crédito	= credit
el escritorio	= office	la correspondencia	= correspondence
el cheque	= cheque		
el billete de banco	= banknote	la muestra	= sample, pattern
		el corresponsal	= correspondent
el almacén	= warehouse; store	el balance	= balance sheet
el reconocimiento	= acknowledgment	la compra	= purchase
		la acción	= share
los intereses	= interest	la aceptación	= acceptance
la tasa	= rate (of interest)	el sello	= stamp
la baja	= fall (in price)	el negociante	= businessman
el alza	= rise (in price)	el cajero	= cashier
el flete	= freight	el agente	= agent
la rebaja	= reduction	el acta	= act, certificate
la garantía	= security, guarantee	el agente de cambio	= stockbroker
el fallido	= bankrupt		

XIV

THE TWELFTH LESSON

THE following extract is not translated as heretofore, but a vocabulary of the most necessary words has been placed at the end of it.

THE BULL-FIGHT [1]

Los tres picadores saludaron al presidente de la plaza precedidos de los banderilleros y chulos, espléndidamente vestidos.

Capitaneaban a todos los primeros espadas y sus sobresalientes, cuyos trajes eran todavía más lujosos que los de aquéllos.

El alcalde hizo la seña; sonaron los clarines, que produjeron un levantamiento general, y entonces se abrió la ancha puerta del toril.

Un toro colorado se precipitó en la arena y fue saludado por una explosión de gritos, de silbidos, de injurias y de elogios.

Al oir este tremendo estrépito, el toro se paró, alzó la cabeza y pareció preguntar con sus encendidos ojos si todas aquellas provocaciones se dirigían a él; reconoció el terreno y volvió precipitadamente la cabeza a uno y otro lado. Todavía vaciló, crecieron los recios silbidos; entonces se precipitó con prontitud hacia el picador.

Pero retrocedió al sentir el dolor que le produjo la puja de la garrocha en el morrillo; no se encarnizó en este primer ataque, sino que embistió al segundo picador.

Éste no le aguardaba tan prevenido como su antecesor; así es que hirió al animal sin detenerlo. Las astas desaparecieron en el cuerpo del caballo que cayó al suelo.

Alzóse un grito de espanto en todo el circo; al punto todos los

---

[1] Fernán Caballero. It is worth noting that this account of a bull-fight was written over a hundred years ago. The technique of the modern 'corrida' is rather different from the one described here.

chulos rodearon aquel grupo horrible; pero el feroz animal se
había apoderado de la presa y no se dejaba distraer de su venganza.

El toro se cebaba en el caballo; el caballo abrumaba con su
peso y sus movimientos convulsivos al picador.

Entonces se vio llegar, sosegado y risueño, a un joven cubierto
de plata, que brillaba como una estrella. Se acercó por detrás del
toro y cogió con sus dos manos la cola de la fiera y la atrajo a sí,
como si hubiese sido un perrito faldero.

Sorprendido el toro, se revolvió furioso contra su adversario,
quien andando hacia atrás, evitó el primer choque con una media
vuelta a la derecha.

El toro volvió a embestir, y el joven lo esquivó segunda vez
con un recorte a la izquierda, siguiendo del mismo modo hasta
llegar cerca de la barrera.

Allí desapareció a los ojos atónitos del animal y a las ansiosas
miradas del público, el cual, ebrio de entusiasmo, atronó los aires
con inmensos aplausos.

El toro había despachado ya un número considerable de
caballos.

Otros, que no habían podido levantarse, yacían tendidos con
las convulsiones de la agonía; a veces alzaban la cabeza, en que se
pintaba la imagen del terror.

A ciertas señales de vida, el toro volvía a la carga hiriendo de
nuevo con sus fieras astas los miembros destrozados de su
víctima.

Después, ensangrentada la frente, se paseaba alrededor del
circo, unas veces alzando la cabeza a las gradas donde la gritería
no cesaba un momento, otras hacia los chulos, que pasaban
delante de él, a manera de meteoros, clavándole las banderillas.

A una señal del presidente, sonaron otra vez los clarines, Pepe
Vera,[1] con una espada y una capa encarnada, se encaminó hacia
el palco del Ayuntamiento,[2] se dirigió al Duque,[3] y quitándose la
montera,

—Brindo,— dijo, —por Vuestra Excelencia, y por la real moza
que tiene a su lado.

[1] A celebrated **matador**.   [2] The municipal council.
[3] President of the fête.

Y al decir esto, arrojó al suelo la montera con inimitable desgaire, y partió adonde su obligación le llamaba.

Agitó la capa que llevaba en la mano izquierda.

El toro le embistió.

Él le pasó de muleta, y en cuanto la fiera volvió a acometerle, le dirigió la espada por entre las dos espaldillas, de modo que el animal, continuando su arranque, ayudó a que todo el hierro penetrase en su cuerpo hasta la empuñadura.

Al mismo tiempo, sonó la música militar.

Pepe Vera atravesó el circo en medio de frenéticos testimonios de aprobación, saludando con la espada sin que excitase en su pecho ni sorpresa ni orgullo un triunfo que más de un emperador romano habría envidiado.

Notes

Saludar means 'to greet, salute, hail'.

Banderilla means 'small decorated dart'.

Banderillero is the bull-fighter who plants the darts in the bull's withers.

Chulo means here 'bull-fighter's assistant'.

Capitanear means 'to command, be in command of'; 'to head, to lead'.

Espada means 'sword' if feminine; 'a swordsman' if masculine.

Sobresaliente is a 'substitute'.

El traje means 'the dress, costume'.

Cuyos means 'whose'; the feminine plural is **cuyas**.

La seña is 'the sign'.

Sonar means 'to sound'.

Clarín means 'bugle'.

Levantamiento means in the above extract 'a rising' (to the feet); it may signify also an 'insurrection' or a 'revolt'.

El toril is the 'place where bulls are kept until needed for the fight'.

Ancha is the feminine form of the adjective **ancho** (wide).

Colorado means 'ruddy, florid'.

Precipitar means 'to precipitate'.

Precipitarse means 'to hurry, dash headlong'.

Grito means 'cry, shout, scream'; the verb is—
Gritar, meaning 'to shout, cry out'.
Silbido means 'whistle, whistling, hiss'; it is derived from the verb—
Silbar, meaning 'to hiss, whistle'.
Injuria means 'insult'.
Elogio means 'eulogy, praise'.
Estrépito means 'noise, clamour'.
Alzar means 'to raise, lift up'.
Preguntar means 'to ask'.
Parecer means 'to seem, appear'.
Dirigir means 'to direct, lead, guide'.
Reconocer means 'to recognize'.
Vacilar means 'to hesitate'.
Crecer means 'to grow, increase'.
Retroceder means 'to retreat'.
Garrocha is 'a pike'.
Morrillo is the part of the neck called the 'nape'.
Encarnizarse means 'to become enraged'.
Embistió is from **embestir,** meaning 'to attack, assail'.
Aguardar means 'to expect, wait'.
Prevenido, from the verb **prevenir,** means 'prepared'; hence also 'forewarned'.
Antecesor means 'predecessor'.
Cayó is from **caer** (to fall).
Espanto means 'fright'.
Rodear means 'to girdle, circle' and 'to wrap up'.
Presa means 'prey'.
Distraer means 'to distract'.
Cebarse en means here 'to tear to pieces'.
Abrumar means 'to oppress, overwhelm'.
Sosegado means 'quiet, calm'.
Risueño means 'smiling'.
Cola means 'tail' and also 'queue'.
Por detrás means 'from behind'.
Fiera means 'wild beast'.
Atrajo comes from **atraer,** meaning 'to attract'.

Perrito faldero [1] means a 'little lap-dog'.

Hacia atrás means 'backwards'.

Evitar means 'to avoid'.

Una media vuelta a la derecha means 'a half turn to the right'.

Esquivar means 'to shun, evade, avoid'.

Atronar means 'to thunder'.

Pintar means 'to paint, picture'.

Hiriendo is the 'gerundio' of **herir**, meaning 'to wound, hurt'.

A la carga means 'at the charge'.

El asta means 'the horn, lance'; it also means 'the handle' of a pencil or brush.

Destrozado is from **destrozar**, meaning 'to destroy'.

Alrededor de means 'around'.

Delante means 'before' and 'in the presence, sight of'.

Clavar means 'to nail, stick, prick'.

Capa means 'cloak'.

Encarnado means 'flesh-coloured, pink, red'.

Encaminarse means 'to make one's way'.

Palco is a 'box' at a theatre or show.

Montera is a 'bull-fighter's cap'.

Brindo is a word used as a kind of toast, or salutation, in bull-fighting.

Arrojar means 'to hurl, throw, launch'.

Pasar de muleta means 'to make a pass with the **muleta** (matador's red cloth)'.

Acometer means 'to attack'.

Arranque (masc.) means 'impetus'.

La empuñadura means 'the hilt'.

El pecho means 'the breast'.

The extract which follows has neither translation nor vocabulary. It will be a useful exercise for practice with the dictionary.

---

[1] **La falda** means 'the skirt, lap'.

CAPTAIN HARVEY [1]

La noche del 17 de marzo de 1870 el *Normandy* hacía su travesía habitual de Southampton a Guernsey.

Una espesa bruma cubría el mar.

El capitán Harvey estaba de pie en la casilla del steamer y maniobraba con precaución, a causa de la noche y de la niebla.

El *Normandy* era un gran buque, el más hermoso quizá de la marina de la Mancha. Seiscientas toneladas, 220 pies ingleses de largo y 25 de ancho.

Era joven, como dicen los marinos; tenía siete años, y había sido construido en 1863.

El capitán Harvey era sobre poco más o menos de la edad que contaba entonces el que escribe estas líneas; tenía patillas blancas, el rostro enérgico y la mirada franca y alegre.

La niebla espesaba, el buque había salido de la ría de Sheerness, estaba en plena mar y avanzaba lentamente.

Eran las cuatro de la mañana.

La oscuridad era absoluta; una especie de nube envolvía el vapor, y apenas se distinguían las puntas de los mástiles.

Nada tan terrible como estos navíos ciegos que avanzan en la noche.

De pronto una masa negra surgió de la bruma.

Fantasma y montañas, promontorio de sombra avanzando sobre la espuma y horadando las tinieblas. Era la *Mary*, gran buque de hélice, procedente de Odesa y que llevaba rumbo a Grimsby, con un cargamento de cien toneladas de grano. Velocidad inmensa, peso enorme. La *Mary* avanza directamente sobre el *Normandy*.

Con tal velocidad se deslizan estos espectros de navíos en la niebla, que no hay medio de evitar el choque. Son encuentros sin aviso; antes que se acabe de verlos se ha muerto.

La *Mary*, lanzada a todo vapor, cogió al *Normandy* por un costado, y le deshizo el casco. La avería producida en ella por el choque la detuvo.

[1] Victor Hugo.

Había en el *Normandy* 28 hombres de tripulación, una mujer de servicio y 21 pasajeros, entre los cuales se contaban 12 mujeres.

La sacudida fue espantosa.

En un instante todos estuvieron en la cubierta, hombres, mujeres y niños, medio desnudos, corriendo, gritando, llorando.

El agua entraba en el interior del buque con furia espantosa.

El combustible de la máquina, apagado por el agua, agonizaba.

El navío no tenía mamparos insumergibles; los cinturones de salvamento faltaban.

El capitán Harvey, de pie sobre la toldilla, gritó, —¡Silencio y atención! Los botes al agua, las mujeres primero, los pasajeros en seguida, la tripulación después. Hay 60 personas que salvar!

Eran 61 pero él se olvidaba de sí.

Los botes fueron echados al agua.

Todos se precipitaron a ellos.

Aquella precipitación podía hacerlos zozobrar.

Ockeleford, el lugarteniente, y los tres contramaestres Goodwin, Bennett y West contuvieron aquella multitud frenética de horror. Dormir y despertar para morir, es espantoso. Sin embargo, por encima de aquellos gritos y de aquel ruido la voz tranquila del capitán, y este breve diálogo se cruzaba en las tinieblas.

—¡Maquinista Locks!

—¡Capitán!

—¿Cómo está la caldera?

—Inundada.

—¿Y el fuego?

—Apagado.

—¿Y la máquina?

—Muerta.

El capitán gritó:

—¡Lugarteniente Ockeleford!

—Presente,— respondió el interpelado.

—¿Con cuántos minutos contamos?

—Con veinte.

—Bastan,— dijo el capitán, —que cada cual se embarque por su turno. Teniente Ockeleford, ¿tenéis pistolas?

—Sí,— contestó.

—Saltad el cráneo a todo hombre que quiera pasar antes que una mujer.

Todos callaron. Nadie se resistió.

La multitud sentíase anonadada por la grandeza de aquella alma.

La *Mary* a su vez había botado sus lanchas al mar y acudía al socorro de los náufragos.

El embarque se operó con orden y casi sin lucha.

Hubo, como siempre, tristes egoísmos; pero también, como siempre, patéticos rasgos de desinterés. Harvey, impasible en su puesto de capitán, mandaba, dominaba, dirigía; se ocupaba de todo y de todos; gobernaba con calma aquella angustia y parecía dar órdenes a la catástrofe.

Se hubiera dicho que el naufragio le obedecía.

A cierto tiempo gritó:

—¡Sálvate, Clemente!

Clemente era el grumete,—un niño.

El buque se sumergía ya en la profundidad de las aguas.

El transbordo del *Normandy* a la *Mary* se hacía cada vez con más rapidez.

—Apresuraos,— murmuró el capitán.

Al expirar los veinte minutos el vapor se eclipsó.

La proa se hundió poco a poco; después la popa.

El capitán Harvey, de pie sobre la toldilla (*quarter-deck*), no hizo un gesto, no pronunció una palabra, y se sumergió en el abismo.

Sólo se vio a través de la bruma la siniestra sombra del buque perderse para siempre.

Tal fue el trágico fin del capitán Harvey.

Que desde el cielo reciba el adiós del que en una ocasión solemne obtuvo hospitalidad en el buque que le sirvió de tumba. Ningún marino de la Mancha le igualaba en grandeza.

Después de haberse impuesto toda su vida el deber de ser un hombre, usó al morir el derecho de ser un héroe.

CLOTHING

el sombrero	= hat		**el sobretodo**	= overcoat
el gorro	= cap		**el pantalón**	= trousers
la bota	= boot		**la capa**	= cloak, cape
la media	= stocking		**el manguito**	= muff
el cuello	= collar		**la manga**	= sleeve
la camisa	= shirt		**la ropa blanca**	= linen
el bolsillo	= pocket		**el encaje**	= lace
la pantufla	= slipper		**la jarretera**	= garter
los guantes	= gloves		**el traje, vestido**	= costume, suit
el pañuelo	= handkerchief		**el calcetín**	= sock
el zapato	= shoe		**los calzoncillos**	= drawers
el delantal	= apron		**los tirantes**	= braces
el velo	= veil		**el botón**	= button
la chaqueta	= jacket			

APPENDICES

APPENDIX I

Examples of the use of **ser** *and* **estar**

ser hombre, soldado, amigo, alemán, francés, inglés, rey, comerciante, jardinero, *etc.*	= to be a man, soldier, friend, German, French, English, king, businessman, gardener, *etc.*
ser fácil, difícil, posible, imposible	= to be easy, difficult, possible, impossible
ser grande, pequeño, bueno, malo, negro, blanco, leal, honroso, *etc.*	= to be big, small, good, bad, black, white, loyal, honest, *etc.*
ser de oro, de hierro, de madera, *etc.*	= to be made of gold, of iron, of wood, *etc.*
ser de Londres, de París, *etc.*	= to be from London, Paris, *etc.*
este jardín es de mi hermano	= this garden is my brother's
esta casa es mía	= this house is mine
esta carta es para Vd.	= this letter is for you
es de desear . . .	= it is to be desired . . .
es decir . . .	= that is to say . . .
es tarde	= it is late
es de día	= it is daytime
es de noche	= it is night-time
es probable que . . .	= it is probable that . . .
es preciso que . . .	= it is necessary that . . .
fue castigado por su padre	= he was punished by his father
los vidrios fueron rotos por la explosión	= the window-panes were broken by the explosion
este actor es bien conocido	= this actor is well known
soy aficionado a la música	= I am fond of music
estar bien	= to be well
estar enfermo	= to be ill
estar triste	= to be sad
estar contento	= to be pleased
estar alegre	= to be cheerful
estar en casa	= to be at home
estar ausente	= to be absent, away
estar de viaje	= to be on a journey
estar limpio, sucio	= to be clean, dirty
estar lleno, vacío	= to be full, empty
está escribiendo una carta	= he is writing a letter
estoy hablando del tiempo	= I am talking about the weather
estar de guardia	= to be on the watch

estar de prisa	= to be in a hurry
estoy seguro de que . . .	= I am sure that . . .
estoy convencido de que . . .	= I am convinced that . . .
estar para salir	= to be on the point of going out
estoy por decir	= I am inclined to say
estoy por él	= I am in favour of him
el tren está para salir	= the train is ready to leave
el tren está por salir	= the train has not left yet
¿cómo está Pedro?	= how is Pedro?
¿cómo es Pedro?	= what is Pedro like?
ser bueno	= to be good
estar bueno	= to be well
ser ciego	= to be blind
está ciego de rabia	= he is blind with rage
ella es guapa	= she is pretty
ella está guapa hoy	= she is looking pretty today
estar cansado	= to be tired
ser cansado	= to be tiresome, wearisome
estar aburrido	= to be bored
ser aburrido	= to be boring

Expressions using tener

tengo hambre	= I am hungry
tenemos sed	= we are thirsty
tiene sueño	= he is sleepy
Vd. tiene razón	= you are right
tengo frío	= I am cold
tenemos calor	= we are hot, warm
tengo para mí que	= it's my opinion that . . .
tengo que ir a la una	= I must go at one o'clock
tiene veinte años	= he is twenty
el cuarto tiene diez metros de largo	= the room is ten metres long
eso no tiene nada que ver conmigo	= that has nothing to do with me
tengo mucho que hacer	= I have a lot to do
tener miedo	= to be afraid
lo tengo muy visto	= I've seen it all before

The Weather

hace calor	= it is hot, warm
hace frío	= it is cold
hace fresco	= it is cool
hace sol	= it is sunny
está nublado	= it is cloudy

llueve, está lloviendo	= it is raining
nieva, está nevando	= it is snowing
hace viento, corre viento	= it is windy
truena	= it is thundering
relampaguea	= it is lightning
truenos y relámpagos	= thunder and lightning

Adverbial Expressions

a veces	= at times, sometimes
de vez en cuando	= from time to time, occasionally
a menudo	= often
rara vez	= rarely
de repente de pronto }	= suddenly
de golpe	
en seguida	= immediately
de propósito	= on purpose
sin querer	= unintentionally
de buena gana	= willingly
de mala gana	= unwillingly, reluctantly
cuanto antes lo más pronto posible }	= as soon as possible
al amanecer	= at dawn
al anochecer	= at nightfall
anoche	= last night
ayer	= yesterday
anteayer	= the day before yesterday
hace tres días	= three days ago
mañana	= tomorrow
pasado mañana	= the day after tomorrow
mañana por la mañana	= tomorrow morning
por la mañana	= in the morning
a las diez de la mañana	= at ten o'clock in the morning
por la noche	= at night
a las diez de la noche	= at ten o'clock at night
de día, de noche	= by day, by night
el mes corriente	= the present month
el mes pasado	= last month
el mes próximo, el mes que viene	= next month
a principios del mes	= at the beginning of the month
a fines del mes	= at the end of the month

Expressions of Comparison

ella es más guapa que su hermana	= she is prettier than her sister
él es menos rico que su hermano	= he is less wealthy than his brother
Vd. tiene más dinero que yo	= you have more money than I
soy tan inteligente como él	= I am as intelligent as he is
él no es tan listo como ella	= he is not as able as she is
es más rico de lo que parece	= he is wealthier than he seems
estas señoras son menos elegantes de lo que eran	= these ladies are less elegant than they were
tiene más dinero del que tenía el año pasado	= he has more money than he had last year
veo menos personas hoy de las que vi ayer	= I see fewer people today than I saw yesterday

APPENDIX II

STUDENTS will probably find it convenient on occasions to be able to consult a list of verbs with all their irregularities detailed on the same page. In the following table the regular verbs are given first, then verbs with minor

Verb

Infinitive	Present Indicative	Present Subjunctive	Past Participle and 'Gerundio'	Imperfect	Preterite
hablar (to speak)	hablo hablas habla hablamos habláis hablan	hable hables hable hablemos habléis hablen	hablado hablando	hablaba hablabas hablaba hablábamos hablabais hablaban	hablé hablaste habló hablamos hablasteis hablaron
temer (to fear)	temo temes teme tememos teméis temen	tema temas tema temamos temáis teman	temido temiendo	temía temías temía temíamos temíais temían	temí temiste temió temimos temisteis temieron
permitir (to permit)	permito permites permite permitimos permitís permiten	permita permitas permita permitamos permitáis permitan	permitido permitiendo	permitía permitías permitía permitíamos permitíais permitían	permití permitiste permitió permitimos permitisteis permitieron
cerrar (to shut)	cierro cierras cierra cerramos cerráis cierran	cierre cierres cierre cerremos cerréis cierren			
contar (to count, to relate)	cuento cuentas cuenta contamos contáis cuentan	cuente cuentes cuente contemos contéis cuenten			
jugar (to play)	juego juegas juega jugamos jugáis juegan	juegue juegues juegue juguemos juguéis jueguen			jugué jugaste jugó jugamos jugasteis jugaron

irregularities, and finally those verbs which are fully irregular, in the sense that, apart from their compounds, they are conjugated like no other verb. The list is not exhaustive, but it contains all the verbs that the student is likely to require in the early stages of learning the language.

Where there is no entry for certain tenses and parts it is to be understood that the verb is conjugated regularly.

Tables

Infinitive	Future	Conditional	Imperfect Subjunctive	Imperative (tú and vosotros)
ablar (to speak)	hablaré hablarás hablará hablaremos hablaréis hablarán	hablaría hablarías hablaría hablaríamos hablaríais hablarían	hablase or hablara hablases or hablaras hablase or hablara hablásemos or habláramos hablaseis or hablarais hablasen or hablaran	habla hablad
emer (to fear)	temeré temerás temerá temeremos temeréis temerán	temería temerías temería temeríamos temeríais temerían	temiese or temiera temieses or temieras temiese or temiera temiésemos or temiéramos temieseis or temierais temiesen or temieran	teme temed
ermitir to permit)	permitiré permitirás permitirá permitiremos permitiréis permitirán	permitiría permitirías permitiría permitiríamos permitiríais permitirían	permitiese or permitiera permitieses or permitieras permitiese or permitiera permitiésemos or permitiéramos permitieseis or permitierais permitiesen or permitieran	permite permitid
rrar to shut)				cierra cerrad
ontar (to count, to relate)				cuenta contad
gar (to play)				juega jugad

Infinitive	Present Indicative	Present Subjunctive	Past Participle and 'Gerundio'	Imperfect	Preterite
perder (to lose)	pierdo pierdes pierde perdemos perdéis pierden	pierda pierdas pierda perdamos perdáis pierdan			
volver (to return)	vuelvo vuelves vuelve volvemos volvéis vuelven	vuelva vuelvas vuelva volvamos volváis vuelvan	vuelto volviendo		
pedir (to ask)	pido pides pide pedimos pedís piden	pida pidas pida pidamos pidáis pidan	pedido pidiendo		pedí pediste pidió pedimos pedisteis pidieron
sentir (to feel)	siento sientes siente sentimos sentís sienten	sienta sientas sienta sintamos sintáis sientan	sentido sintiendo		sentí sentiste sintió sentimos sentisteis sintieron
dormir (to sleep)	duermo duermes duerme dormimos dormís duermen	duerma duermas duerma durmamos durmáis duerman	dormido durmiendo		dormí dormiste durmió dormimos dormisteis durmieron
buscar (to look for)		busque busques busque busquemos busquéis busquen			busqué buscaste buscó buscamos buscasteis buscaron
llegar (to arrive)		llegue llegues llegue lleguemos lleguéis lleguen			llegué llegaste llegó llegamos llegasteis llegaron
rezar (to pray)		rece reces rece recemos recéis recen			recé rezaste rezó rezamos rezasteis rezaron
averiguar (to verify)		averigüe averigües averigüe averigüemos averigüéis averigüen			averigüé averiguaste averiguó averiguamos averiguasteis averiguaron

Infinitive	Future	Conditional	Imperfect Subjunctive	Imperative (tú and vosotros)
erder (to lose)				pierde perded
olver (to return)				vuelve volved
edir (to ask)			pidiese *or* pidiera pidieses *or* pidieras pidiese *or* pidiera pidiésemos *or* pidiéramos pidieseis *or* pidierais pidiesen *or* pidieran	pide pedid
ntir (to feel)			sintiese *or* sintiera sintieses *or* sintieras sintiese *or* sintiera sintiésemos *or* sintiéramos sintieseis *or* sintierais sintiesen *or* sintieran	siente sentid
ormir (to sleep)			durmiese *or* durmiera durmieses *or* durmieras durmiese *or* durmiera durmiésemos *or* durmiéramos durmieseis *or* durmierais durmiesen *or* durmieran	duerme dormid
ascar (to look for)				
egar (to arrive)				
zar (to pray)				
eriguar (to verify)				

Infinitive	Present Indicative	Present Subjunctive	Past Participle and 'Gerundio'	Imperfect	Preterite
vencer (to conquer)	venzo vences vence vencemos vencéis vencen	venza venzas venza venzamos venzáis venzan			
coger (to catch)	cojo coges coge cogemos cogéis cogen	coja cojas coja cojamos cojáis cojan			
conocer (to know)	conozco conoces conoce conocemos conocéis conocen	conozca conozcas conozca conozcamos conozcáis conozcan			
esparcir (to scatter)	esparzo esparces esparce esparcimos esparcís esparcen	esparza esparzas esparza esparzamos esparzáis esparzan			
dirigir (to direct)	dirijo diriges dirige dirigimos dirigís dirigen	dirija dirijas dirija dirijamos dirijáis dirijan			
distinguir (to distinguish)	distingo distingues distingue distinguimos distinguís distinguen	distinga distingas distinga distingamos distingáis distingan			
delinquir (to offend)	delinco delinques delinque delinquimos delinquís delinquen	delinca delincas delinca delincamos delincáis delincan			
lucir (to shine)	luzco luces luce lucimos lucís lucen	luzca luzcas luzca luzcamos luzcáis luzcan			
variar (to vary)	varío varías varía variamos variáis varían	varíe varíes varíe variemos variéis varíen			

Infinitive	Future	Conditional	Imperfect Subjunctive	Imperative (tú and vosotros)
ncer (to conquer)				
ger (to catch)				
nocer (to know)				
parcir (to scatter)				
igir (to direct)				
stinguir (to distinguish)				
linquir (to offend)				
cir (to shine)				
riar (to vary)				

Infinitive	Present Indicative	Present Subjunctive	Past Participle and 'Gerundio'	Imperfect	Preterite
valuar (to value)	valúo valúas valúa valuamos valuáis valúan	valúe valúes valúe valuemos valuéis valúen			
leer (to read)			leído leyendo		leí leíste leyó leímos leísteis leyeron
construir (to build)	construyo construyes construye construimos construís construyen	construya construyas construya construyamos construyáis construyan	construido construyendo		construí construiste construyó construimo construiste construyerc
andar (to walk)					anduve anduviste anduvo anduvimos anduvisteis anduvieron
dar (to give)	doy das da damos dais dan	dé des dé demos deis den			di diste dio dimos disteis dieron
estar (to be)	estoy estás está estamos estáis están	esté estés esté estemos estéis estén			estuve estuviste estuvo estuvimos estuvisteis estuvieron
caber (to be contained)	quepo cabes cabe cabemos cabéis caben	quepa quepas quepa quepamos quepáis quepan			cupe cupiste cupo cupimos cupisteis cupieron
caer (to fall)	caigo caes cae caemos caéis caen	caiga caigas caiga caigamos caigáis caigan	caído cayendo		caí caíste cayó caímos caísteis cayeron
haber (to have)	he has ha hemos habéis han	haya hayas haya hayamos hayáis hayan			hube hubiste hubo hubimos hubisteis hubieron

Infinitive	Future	Conditional	Imperfect Subjunctive	Imperative (tú and vosotros)
aluar (to value)				
er (to read)			leyese or leyera leyeses or leyeras leyese or leyera leyésemos or leyéramos leyeseis or leyerais leyesen or leyeran	
nstruir (to build)			construyese or construyera construyeses or construyeras construyese or construyera construyésemos or construyéramos construyeseis or construyerais construyesen or construyeran	construye construid
dar (to walk)			anduviese or anduviera anduvieses or anduvieras anduviese or anduviera anduviésemos or anduviéramos anduvieseis or anduvierais anduviesen or anduvieran	
r (to give)			diese or diera dieses or dieras diese or diera diésemos or diéramos dieseis or dierais diesen or dieran	
tar (to be)			estuviese or estuviera estuvieses or estuvieras estuviese or estuviera estuviésemos or estuviéramos estuvieseis or estuvierais estuviesen or estuvieran	estate estad
ber (to be contained)	cabré cabrás cabrá cabremos cabréis cabrán	cabría cabrías cabría cabríamos cabríais cabrían	cupiese or cupiera cupieses or cupieras cupiese or cupiera cupiésemos or cupiéramos cupieseis or cupierais cupiesen or cupieran	
r (to fall)			cayese or cayera cayeses or cayeras cayese or cayera cayésemos or cayéramos cayeseis or cayerais cayesen or cayeran	
ber (to have)	habré habrás habrá habremos habréis habrán	habría habrías habría habríamos habríais habrían	hubiese or hubiera hubieses or hubieras hubiese or hubiera hubiésemos or hubiéramos hubieseis or hubierais hubiesen or hubieran	

Infinitive	Present Indicative	Present Subjunctive	Past Participle and 'Gerundio'	Imperfect	Preterite
hacer (to do, make)	hago haces hace hacemos hacéis hacen	haga hagas haga hagamos hagáis hagan	hecho haciendo		hice hiciste hizo hicimos hicisteis hicieron
poder (to be able)	puedo puedes puede podemos podéis pueden	pueda puedas pueda podamos podáis puedan	podido pudiendo		pude pudiste pudo pudimos pudisteis pudieron
poner (to put)	pongo pones pone ponemos ponéis ponen	ponga pongas ponga pongamos pongáis pongan	puesto poniendo		puse pusiste puso pusimos pusisteis pusieron
querer (to want)	quiero quieres quiere queremos queréis quieren	quiera quieras quiera queramos queráis quieran			quise quisiste quiso quisimos quisisteis quisieron
saber (to know)	sé sabes sabe sabemos sabéis saben	sepa sepas sepa sepamos sepáis sepan			supe supiste supo supimos supisteis supieron
ser (to be)	soy eres es somos sois son	sea seas sea seamos seáis sean		era eras era éramos erais eran	fui fuiste fue fuimos fuisteis fueron
tener to have)	tengo tienes tiene tenemos tenéis tienen	tenga tengas tenga tengamos tengáis tengan			tuve tuviste tuvo tuvimos tuvisteis tuvieron
traer (to bring)	traigo traes trae traemos traéis traen	traiga traigas traiga traigamos traigáis traigan	traído trayendo		traje trajiste trajo trajimos trajisteis trajeron
valer (to be worth)	valgo vales vale valemos valéis valen	valga valgas valga valgamos valgáis valgan			

Infinitive	Future	Conditional	Imperfect Subjunctive	Imperative (tú and vosotros)
acer (to do, make)	haré harás hará haremos haréis harán	haría harías haría haríamos haríais harían	hiciese or hiciera hicieses or hicieras hiciese or hiciera hiciésemos or hiciéramos hicieseis or hicierais hiciesen or hicieran	haz haced
oder (to be able)	podré podrás podrá podremos podréis podrán	podría podrías podría podríamos podríais podrían	pudiese or pudiera pudieses or pudieras pudiese or pudiera pudiésemos or pudiéramos pudieseis or pudierais pudiesen or pudieran	
oner (to put)	pondré pondrás pondrá pondremos pondréis pondrán	pondría pondrías pondría pondríamos pondríais pondrían	pusiese or pusiera pusieses or pusieras pusiese or pusiera pusiésemos or pusiéramos pusieseis or pusierais pusiesen or pusieran	pon poned
uerer (to want)	querré querrás querrá querremos querréis querrán	querría querrías querría querríamos querríais querrían	quisiese or quisiera quisieses or quisieras quisiese or quisiera quisiésemos or quisiéramos quisieseis or quisierais quisiesen or quisieran	
ber (to know)	sabré sabrás sabrá sabremos sabréis sabrán	sabría sabrías sabría sabríamos sabríais sabrían	supiese or supiera supieses or supieras supiese or supiera supiésemos or supiéramos supieseis or supierais supiesen or supieran	
r (to be)			fuese or fuera fueses or fueras fuese or fuera fuésemos or fuéramos fueseis or fuerais fuesen or fueran	sé sed
ner (to have)	tendré tendrás tendrá tendremos tendréis tendrán	tendría tendrías tendría tendríamos tendríais tendrían	tuviese or tuviera tuvieses or tuvieras tuviese or tuviera tuviésemos or tuviéramos tuvieseis or tuvierais tuviesen or tuvieran	ten tened
aer (to bring)			trajese or trajera trajeses or trajeras trajese or trajera trajésemos or trajéramos trajeseis or trajerais trajesen or trajeran	
ler (to be worth)	valdré valdrás valdrá valdremos valdréis valdrán	valdría valdrías valdría valdríamos valdríais valdrían		

Infinitive	Present Indicative	Present Subjunctive	Past Participle and 'Gerundio'	Imperfect	Preterite
ver (to see)	veo ves ve vemos veis ven	vea veas vea veamos veáis vean	visto viendo	veía veías veía veíamos veíais veían	vi viste vio vimos visteis vieron
conducir (to lead, drive)	conduzco conduces conduce conducimos conducís conducen	conduzca conduzcas conduzca conduzcamos conduzcáis conduzcan			conduje condujiste condujo condujimos condujisteis condujeron
asir (to grasp)	asgo ases ase asimos asís asen	asga asgas asga asgamos asgáis asgan			
decir (to say, tell)	digo dices dice decimos decís dicen	diga digas diga digamos digáis digan	dicho diciendo		dije dijiste dijo dijimos dijisteis dijeron
ir (to go)	voy vas va vamos vais van	vaya vayas vaya vayamos vayáis vayan	ido yendo	iba ibas iba íbamos ibais iban	fui fuiste fue fuimos fuisteis fueron
oir (to hear)	oigo oyes oye oímos oís oyen	oiga oigas oiga oigamos oigáis oigan	oído oyendo		oí oíste oyó oímos oísteis oyeron
reir (to laugh)	río ríes ríe reímos reís ríen	ría rías ría riamos riais rían	reído riendo		reí reíste rió reímos reísteis rieron
salir (to go out)	salgo sales sale salimos salís salen	salga salgas salga salgamos salgáis salgan			
venir (to·come)	vengo vienes viene venimos venís vienen	venga vengas venga vengamos vengáis vengan	venido viniendo		vine viniste vino vinimos vinisteis vinieron

Infinitive	Future	Conditional	Imperfect Subjunctive	Imperative (tú and vosotros)
ᵉr (to see)				
nducir (to lead, drive)			condujese *or* condujera condujeses *or* condujeras condujese *or* condujera condujésemos *or* condujéramos condujeseis *or* condujerais condujesen *or* condujeran	
ᵉir (to grasp)				
ᵉcir (to say, tell)	diré dirás dirá diremos diréis dirán	diría dirías diría diríamos diríais dirían	dijese *or* dijera dijeses *or* dijeras dijese *or* dijera dijésemos *or* dijéramos dijeseis *or* dijerais dijesen *or* dijeran	di decid
(to go)			fuese *or* fuera fueses *or* fueras fuese *or* fuera fuésemos *or* fuéramos fueseis *or* fuerais fuesen *or* fueran	ve id
ᵉr (to hear)			oyese *or* oyera oyeses *or* oyeras oyese *or* oyera oyésemos *or* oyéramos oyeseis *or* oyerais oyesen *or* oyeran	oye oíd
ᵉir (to laugh)			riese *or* riera rieses *or* rieras riese *or* riera riésemos *or* riéramos rieseis *or* rierais riesen *or* rieran	ríe reíd
ᵉlir (to go out)	saldré saldrás saldrá saldremos saldréis saldrán	saldría saldrías saldría saldríamos saldríais saldrían		sal salid
nir (to come)	vendré vendrás vendrá vendremos vendréis vendrán	vendría vendrías vendría vendríamos vendríais vendrían	viniese *or* viniera vinieses *or* vinieras viniese *or* viniera viniésemos *or* viniéramos vinieseis *or* vinierais viniesen *or* vinieran	ven venid

NOTES

NOTES

NOTES